DIRECTORY OF TEST COLLECTIONS IN

ACADEMIC, PROFESSIONAL, AND RESEARCH LIBRARIES

EDITED BY

Paul G. Fehrmann and Nancy Patricia O'Brien

COMPILED BY

Ad hoc Committee on the Test Collection Directory
Education and Behavior Sciences Section
Association of College and Research Libraries

Directory of Test Collections in Academic, Professional, and Research Libraries

Edited by

Paul G. Fehrmann and Nancy Patricia O'Brien

Compiled by

Ad hoc Committee on the Test Collection Directory
Education and Behavioral Sciences Section
Association of College and Research Libraries

Data Analyzed, Collated, Formatted, and Indexed by

Cheryl R. Sturko Grossman

Association of College and Research Libraries
A division of the American Library Association
Chicago, 2001

The paper used in this publication meets the minimum requirements of American National Standard for Information Sciences–Permanence of Paper for Printed Library Materials, ANSI Z39.48-1992. ∞

Library of Congress Cataloging-in-Publication Data
Directory of test collections in academic, professional, and research
libraries / edited by Paul G. Fehrmann and Nancy Patricia O'Brien ;
compiled by Ad Hoc Committee on the Test Collection Directory, Education
and Behavioral Sciences Section, Association of College and Research
Libraries ; directory data analyzed, collated, formatted, and indexed by
Cheryl R. Sturko Grossman.
     p. cm.
Includes bibliographical references and index.
  ISBN 0-8389-8167-4 (alk. paper)
1. Educational tests and measurements--United States--Library
resources--Directories. 2. Examinations--United States--Library
resources--Directories. I. Fehrmann, Paul G. II. O'Brien, Nancy P. III.
Grossman, Cheryl R. Sturko. IV. Association of College and Research
Libraries. Ad Hoc Committee on the Test Collection Directory.
  LB3051 .D564 2001
  371.26'025'73--dc21

                 2001004554

Printed on recycled paper.

Printed in the United States of America.

05 04 03 02   5 4 3 2

Contents

Introduction

Researchers and practitioners often need to identify, locate and examine tests that might be used for their work. However, accessing tests for purposes of reviewing them can be problematic. Despite many efforts to bring some sense of organization to the management and awareness of test collections in libraries and other institutions, there has been an ongoing need for a systematic survey of the collections available to researchers and practitioners who need to know the content of various tests. That is, since most tests have restrictions placed on their use and accessibility by publishers, it is often possible to review tests only when affiliated with a particular institution or program that maintains a test collection. At the same time, many professionals do not have the financial resources to buy expensive tests simply to examine them for possible adoption in a particular setting. Instead, these test users seek collections where they can look over a number of tests and determine which best fit their needs. Once that decision is made, they can then purchase the number of copies needed for the testing program. Similarly, researchers who are examining tests for their content and design may not be able to invest in the purchase of many expensive tests, but seek a repository that will provide them with an array of current, and sometimes historical test materials. Because of the publisher restrictions on test use and accessibility, there are only a relatively small number of locations in the U.S. that offer these materials for review. This directory is an attempt to provide a list of institutions that will allow access to their test collections.

Development of the Directory

Recognizing the need for researchers and practitioners to have a list of those institutions that have a significant collection of tests and/or make their test collections accessible onsite, the Psychology/Psychiatry Committee of the Education and Behavioral Sciences Section (EBSS) of the Association of College and Research Libraries proposed that an ad hoc committee be formed to compile a directory of these special, under-publicized collections. Once approval was received from the EBSS Executive Committee, a committee was appointed in 1997 that included members from the Psychology/Psychiatry Committee as well as other interested EBSS members. Paul Fehrmann and Nancy O'Brien were appointed co-chairs. At its initial meeting, the committee determined that in order to be useful the directory should meet the following criteria: include those collections which were located at institutions that permitted access to the collection by more than departmental constituents, and list collections with more than 100 tests. A key consideration was improving awareness of those test collections that permitted affiliated or other researchers to examine the materials in the collections. If a collection could not meet this criterion, it was not considered for inclusion. Similarly, it was felt that emphasis would be given to collections with 100 or more tests. A collection of fewer than 100 tests would most likely contain well known and easily accessible tests available to researchers through local counseling programs or school districts. However, during the process of compiling the directory data, it was decided that inclusion of even the smaller collections of tests would be useful for the researcher seeking test information.

In order to compile this directory, a pilot survey was developed and was sent using electronic mail to a select few sites. The responses were used to modify the form further, and to refine those questions that appeared to be problematic. A final version of the form and the cover letter can be found in Appendix A.

The survey solicited descriptive and quantitative information such as address, size of collection, availability, contents and focus of collection, and general information of interest to potential users. The inclusion of historical components, such as tests that had been superseded by newer editions, or tests that were no longer in print was considered important enough information for researchers to be listed as a separate question on the survey.

The survey was sent to targeted institutions that were either known to have test collections, or which seemed likely to have test collections. The list of institutions was compiled from the following sources. An estimate of the number of contacts identified in each source is indicated in parentheses. Ash's *Subject Collections* (30), *College Blue Book* (284) and the *Directory of Curriculum Materials Centers*, 1996 (279) were the print sources used. Additionally, listservs were used to send out surveys to other groups and organizations that were identified as likely recipients. These included the Education and Behavioral Sciences Section listserv (197), 3 listservs from the Special Libraries Association—Divisions for Education; Biomedical and Life Sciences; and Social Sciences (1,451), and the National Council of Schools and Programs of Professional Psychology (62). Individual messages were sent to the Buros Institute of Mental Measurements Library (1), the Educational Testing Service Library (1) and the American College Testing Program (1).

Each committee member was assigned to distribute selected surveys via e-mail during late spring 1999. As they were received, each one of the surveys was checked to verify completeness. As needed, requests for clarification or follow-up requests were also sent. At the same time, committee member Cheryl Grossman had been identified to serve as the collator for the contents of the directory. Each committee member was directed to send responses to her for formatting and entry into a pre-determined template.

During the summer 1999 meeting, committee members also decided that the following indexes should be included if there were sufficient entries in each to merit a separate index. These indexes were identified as those that would indicate collections having restricted access and use; listing by size; those that had historical collections; those that included *Tests in Microfiche* (*TIM*); those that were searchable via a database or online catalog; and listing by collection strengths. The reason for listing *TIM* in a separate index was due to its availability for reproduction. *TIM* consists of unpublished research instruments, with less stringent restrictions on reproduction than those instituted by test publishers. *TIM* offers a useful alternative to the student or researcher needing a reproducible test, since basic copyright guidelines apply, and in some instances direct permission is included for educational copying.

The primary organization of the entries had already been determined to be geographic by state, and then by name of institution.

Graphs providing information about the different users of tests, about the types of tests used, as well as the number of tests added annually to collections, can be found in the appendixes.

How to Use the Directory

In general, users of this directory will first identify collections of potential use. Next, the user will contact staff working with the identified collections to ask questions and/or to make arrangements for accessing test materials.

As a starting point, the overall organization of entries in this directory is geographic by state, allowing users to determine easily which collections might require the least amount of travel to use. All entries also include broad indications of collection strength (e.g., achievement, behavior assessment, intelligence and scholastic aptitude, personality, reading, etc.) allowing for an additional quick decision concerning relevancy for a given project.

In addition to collection strengths, for each collection site there is also collection size and Internet address information as well as policy information indicating who may use the collection (e.g., students, faculty, outside researchers, general public), and how the materials may be used (e.g., in-house use, check-out to faculty-students, check-out with written approval). Other data such as type of institution, number of test titles added per year, source and amount of budget for tests, and staff time allotted for test collection activities, appear as graphs in the appendixes.

A number of indexes are also provided at the back of this directory, and each index entry includes the page number of the related test collection. Indexes included are as follows: collections with restricted use, test collections by size, collections with historical materials, collections with *Tests in Microfiche*, collections searchable via online catalog/database, and test collections by collection strengths.

Contact information is available for each collection, including name and address, phone number, as well as e-mail and fax, if available. Researchers wishing to use materials at a particular site should contact that site first to determine current policies regarding accessibility, hours of availability, and specific contents of the collection.

Conclusion

Because so many of the currently available resources related to test collections are from the 1980s, and because only a few of those attempted to list significant test collections, the need for an updated directory of test collections is apparent. Researchers seeking to find current test materials or collections having historical components will benefit from this directory. Librarians and information specialists attempting to assist users in finding repositories of these specialized materials can better inform users of local policies and accessibility by use of this directory. This directory will serve as a much needed and valuable guide to materials frequently in demand, but often difficult to track down. **Researchers wishing to use materials at a particular site should contact that site first to determine current policies regarding accessibility, hours of availability and specific contents of the collection.**

Following this introduction is a list of sources that may be helpful to those seeking information about tests, as well as a bibliography of sources that discuss test collections or that were used to identify institutions having test collections.

As always, any omissions or errors are unintentional, and the editors will gladly receive comments in order to insure accuracy in any future editions.

Contributors

The Ad hoc Committee on the Test Collection Directory included the following members, all of whom were active contributors to this project:

Daniel E. Burgard
University of North Texas Health Science Center at Fort Worth
dburgard@hsc.unt.edu

Annette Curtis-Carroll
Western Connecticut State University
curtis@wcsu.ctstateu.edu

Paul G. Fehrmann
Kent State University
pfehrman@lms.kent.edu

Bee Gallegos
Arizona State University West
BeeGallegos@asu.edu

Cheryl R. Sturko Grossman
ERIC Clearinghouse on Adult, Career, and Vocational Education
The Ohio State University
grossman.4@osu.edu

Rolland H. McGiverin
Indiana State University
Libgilb@isugw.indstate.edu

Nancy Patricia O'Brien
University of Illinois at Urbana-Champaign
n-obrien@uiuc.edu

Betsy Simpson
University of Florida
betsys@mail.uflib.ufl.edu

Ted Wygant
Daytona Beach Community College
wygantt@dbcc.cc.fl.us

Further Sources of Information

American College Testing (ACT)
http://www.act.org
As a key organization in the field of educational assessment and career planning, ACT seeks to provide support for students, educators, workers, and employers. Programs and services are designed to serve all individuals, whether their plans include continuing education, vocational training, or entering the workforce. ACT's major assessment tool, the ACT Assessment, is designed to assess high school students' general educational development and their ability to complete college-level work. Components of this assessment cover four skill areas: English, mathematics, reading, and science reasoning.

American Educational Research Association, American Psychological Association, National Council on Measurement in Education.
Standards for Educational and Psychological Testing. Washington, D.C.: American Educational Research Association, 1999.
This is a greatly expanded and revised edition of the 1985 *Standards* covering professional and technical issues of test development and test use in education, psychology and employment. It includes information about latest changes in federal law and measurement trends affecting validity; testing individuals with disabilities or different linguistic backgrounds; and new types of tests as well as new uses of existing tests.

Annual: Volume 1, Training and Volume 2, Consulting. San Francisco, Calif.: Jossey-Bass/Pfeiffer, 1972– .
Formerly published as *A Handbook of Structured Experiences for Human Relations Training* and *The Annual for Group Facilitators*, these annual volumes provide practical information for trainers and consultants in human resources. Each volume includes a section with inventories, questionnaires, and surveys. Materials in the *Annual* volumes may be duplicated for educational and training purposes.

Association of Test Publishers
http://www.testpublishers.org
Represents providers of tests and assessment tools and/or services related to assessment, selection, screening, certification, licensing, educational or clinical uses. Promotes the use of properly developed and appropriately used tests and awareness of and compliance with laws regarding copyrights, trademarks and other intellectual property rights.

Bearden, William O., and Richard G. Netemeyer. *Handbook of Marketing Scales: Multi-item Measures for Marketing and Consumer Behavior Research.* 2nd ed. Thousand Oaks, Calif.: Sage Publications, 1999.
This resource covers multi-item scales used in marketing and consumer behavior survey research. Includes the scale construct, description, development, samples, validity, scores, other evidence, other sources, references, the actual scale items, and, where applicable, directions for using the scale.

Beere, Carole A. *Gender Roles: A Handbook of Tests and Measures.* New York: Greenwood Press, 1990.

A total of 211 measures are found in this resource, with entries including title, author or authors as listed in the earliest publication mentioning the scale, earliest date that the scale is mentioned in a publication, profile of variable being measured, type of instrument, description, sample items, previous and appropriate subjects, scoring information, a description of the development of the measure, information regarding reliability and validity, and a listing of published studies that use the measure. Seven organizing chapters are gender roles, children's gender roles, stereotypes, marital and parental roles, employee roles, multiple roles, and attitudes toward gender role issues. Indexes include scale titles, scale authors, variables measured, and scale users.

———. *Sex and Gender Issues: A Handbook of Tests and Measures.* New York: Greenwood Press. 1990.
Describes nearly 200 scales in detail, providing reliability, validity, and availability information. Tests are organized into eleven chapters on topics such as hetero-social relations and sexuality. Four indexes are included: scale titles, authors, variables measured, and scale users.

Bruner, Gordon C., and Paul J. Hensel. *Marketing Scales Handbook: A Compilation of Multi-item Measures.* 2 volumes. Chicago: American Marketing Association, 1992– .
These two volumes contain descriptions and information for approximately 1,000 multi-item measurement scales that were used in marketing research published during the 1980s and first half of the 1990's. The handbook facilitates the development of questionnaires by providing examples of previously used scales and their psychometric characteristics. It lists the scale's name, its description and origin, samples, the scale's reliability and validity, the manner in which the scale was administered to a sample, the results associated with the scale, comments, references, and the items of each scale. A third volume is expected to cover scales published from 1994 on, and a CD-ROM of all contents (volumes 1–3) is also expected.

Buros Institute of Mental Measurements
http://www.unl.edu/buros
This resource for users of commercially available tests provides guidance on test selection, utilization, and practice. Publishes the *Mental Measurements Yearbook* and *Tests in Print* series.

Corcoran, Kevin and Joel Fischer. *Measures for Clinical Practice: A Source Book.* 3rd ed. 2 volumes. New York: Free Press, 2000.
These volumes include over 400 "rapid assessment instruments" (under 50 items), reviewed in the literature from 1964 to 1999. Measures are for work with couples, families and children (volume 1) and for work with adults (volume 2). Tests are cross-indexed by problem area (e.g., Anger, Identity, Sexuality) in the table of contents.

Directory of Unpublished Experimental Mental Measures. Washington, D.C.: American Psychological Association, 1974– .
This directory of test instruments provides ready access to sources of information about experimental non-standardized mental measures that are undergoing development and are currently not marketed commercially.

Educational Testing Service (ETS)
http://www.ets.org
This preeminent nonprofit company develops and annually administers millions of tests, as they serve the needs of individuals, educational institutions and agencies, and governmental bodies around the world. Major tests include SAT, SAT II, PSAT, AP exams, The Praxis Series: Professional Assessments for Beginning Teachers and Pre-Professional Skills Tests, NAEP: National Assessment of Educational Progress, TOEFL: Test of English as a Foreign Language (paper and computer-based versions), GRE Graduate Record Examinations General Test (paper and computer-based versions), and the GMAT: Graduate Management Admission Test.

ERIC Clearinghouse on Assessment and Evaluation. *ERIC/AE Test Locator* (Includes the ETS Test File, Buros Test Review Locator, Pro-Ed Test Review Locator, and Pro-Ed Test Publisher Locator)
http://www.ericae.net/testcol.htm
The Test Locator, which indexes test instruments in the ETS Test Collection, Buros Test Review Locator, Pro-Ed Test Publisher Locator and Pro-Ed Test Review Locator, is part of a major federally funded assessment resource site by ETS. The main site offers links to virtually every reliable assessment site available, provides full-text of many journal articles and research reports, and is a source for searching the ERIC database, including a list of ERIC descriptors.

FAQ/Finding information about psychological tests" (American Psychological Association Science Directorate)
http://www.apa.org/science/faq-findtests.html
This resource developed by the American Psychological Association provides basic guidance on the following: finding information on a particular test; finding a particular type of test; locating a specific test; locating test publishers; purchasing tests; test references; available software and scoring services; and, additional information on the proper use of tests.

Gallo, Joseph J., et al. *Handbook of Geriatric Assessment.* 3rd ed. Gaithersburg, Md.: Aspen, 1999.
This work seeks to guide evaluation of the older person, including assessment of mental status, function, social situation, physical examination, and health promotion and disease prevention. It includes coverage of issues such as ethnicity in geriatric assessment, the older driver, and assessment in special settings. It also presents a case study of a geriatric assessment program at a university hospital. It is meant for health care professionals, social workers, and researchers working with a wide variety of elderly populations including hospitalized elderly, nursing home residents, and those receiving home care services

Handbook of Sexuality-related Measures. Edited by Clive M. Davis ... [et al.] Thousand Oaks, Calif.: Sage Publications, 1998.
This resource includes hundreds of measures related to a wide variety of variables and topics in the areas of sexual behavior, beliefs, and attitudes. For most tests there is a brief introduction and test description, as well as information on response mode and timing, scoring, reliability, and validity. Each entry also includes references and in most cases, there is a copy of the test.

Health and Psychosocial Instruments (HAPI) CD. [computer file]. Pittsburgh, Pa.: Behavioral Measurement Database Services, 1983–.
With coverage from 1985 to date, HAPI contains information about research and survey instruments such as questionnaires, checklists, rating scales, and interview forms. Topics covered include public health, communication, psychology, nursing, organizational behavior, medicine, sociology, physical education, psychiatry, human resources, gerontology and dental medicine.

Innovations in Clinical Practice. Sarasota, Fla.: Professional Resource Exchange, 1982–.
Each annual volume includes a variety of information useful to mental health practitioners in clinical settings, including forms and informal instruments to assist clinicians in gathering data about clients. Most test instruments may be reproduced for "noncommercial professional or educational use." An index to Volumes 1–17 (1982–1999) is available in print and may be downloaded in ASCII format from the publisher's web site <http://www.prpress.com>.

Joint Committee on Testing Practices, American Psychological Association.
http://www.apa.org/science/jctpweb.html
JCTP provides a means by which professional organizations and test publishers can work together to improve the use of tests in assessment and appraisal. Their activities include providing guidance to professionals who develop or use educational tests; developing educational material relating to the many uses of testing in schools; and, training professionals to use tests wisely.

Joint Committee on Testing Practices, American Psychological Association. *Code of Fair Testing Practices in Education.* Washington, D.C.: Joint Committee on Testing Practices, 1988.
The code is a statement of the primary obligations that professionals who develop or use educational tests have toward test takers.

Jones, Reginald L. *Handbook of Tests and Measurements for Black Populations*, 2 vol. Hampton, Va.: Cobb & Henry Publishers, 1996.
Over 100 instruments and approaches are covered in this two volume work, in sections on infants, children, adolescents, parents, and family structure and dynamics. Each entry provides the instrument's purpose and description, possible uses, appropriate age ranges, administration, reliability and validity and references. A good number of actual tests are also included.

Lester, Paula E., and Lloyd K. Bishop. *Handbook of Tests and Measurement in Education and the Social Sciences.* Lancaster, Pa.: Technomic, 1997.
This handbook contains over 80 actual instruments arranged in 32 categories, along with specific psychometric information and a list of references for each. Adequate support for the reliability and validity of each instrument was the criteria for inclusion.

Lichtenberg, Peter A. *Handbook of Assessment in Clinical Gerontology.* New York: Wiley, 1999.
This handbook provides guidelines on assessing functioning in older adults in areas such as dementia, mental health, depression, anxiety and ability to engage in self-care. Chap-

ters include real clinical and case examples as well as assessment measures and/or sample items. The handbook addresses different settings and situations such as community living, assisted living, long-term care facilities, primary care and hospital settings, and ethnic and cultural diversity.

McDowell, Ian, and Claire Newell. *Measuring Health: A Guide to Rating Scales and Questionnaires*. 2nd ed. New York: Oxford University Press, 1996.
Eighty-eight measurements that evaluate health via questionnaires or rating scales are reviewed in this resource. The description of each method covers its purpose and conceptual basis, its reliability and validity, and a copy of the scale is shown. Measurements covered pertain to areas of physical disability, social health, psychological well-being, depression, mental status, pain, general health status, and quality of life. Subject index is included.

Maddox, Taddy. *Tests: A Comprehensive Reference for Assessments in Psychology, Education, and Business*. 4th ed. Austin, Tex.: Pro-Ed, 1997.
This guide provides quick access to current test information in an easy-to-read format. It contains consistent codified information describing and cataloging tests available for use by psychologists, educators and human resource personnel.

Mental Measurements Yearbook (MMY). Lincoln, Neb.: The Buros Institute of Mental Measurements, The University of Nebraska-Lincoln. 1938– .
Published in alternate years with its supplement, each *MMY* lists new or newly revised commercially available tests in English together with critical reviews by well-qualified professionals and references "related to the development, psychometric quality, and use of specific tests." *MMY* includes indexes of titles, acronyms, names, and scores, a directory and index to publishers, and a classified subject index. See also: *Tests in Print*.

The National Council on Measurement in Education (NCME)
http://ncme.ed.uiuc.edu/
The National Council on Measurement in Education (NCME) is a professional organization for individuals involved in assessment, evaluation, testing, and other aspects of educational measurement. Member activities have involved construction and use of standardized tests; new forms of assessment, including performance-based assessment; program design; and program evaluation. Members include university faculty; test developers; state and federal testing and research directors; professional evaluators; testing specialists in business, industry, education, community programs, and other professions; licensure, certification, and credentialing professionals; graduate students from educational, psychological, and other measurement programs; and others involved in testing issues and practices.

Ostrow, Andrew C. *Directory of Psychological Tests in the Sport and Exercise Sciences*. 2nd ed. Morgantown, W.Va.: Fitness Information Technology, Inc., 1996.
This resource provides coverage of 314 primarily non-commercial tests developed for research as opposed to diagnostic purposes. Test summaries contain sections on purpose, description, construction, reliability, validity, norms, availability, references, and as available, e-mail addresses and phone/fax numbers of each principal test author. Topics in-

clude exercise motivation, sport motivation, aggression, cognitive strategies, leadership, cohesion, and anxiety. Subject, test author, test title and test acronyms indexes are also provided.

Robinson, John P., Phillip R. Shaver, and Lawrence S. Wrightsman. *Measures of Personality and Social Psychological Attitudes*. San Diego, Calif.: Academic Press, 1991.
A comprehensive guide to attitude and personality scales. Entries for tests include a description, discussions of the sample studies, the test's reliability and validity, and a section of results and comments. In cases where copyright permission was obtained, all or some of the test is reprinted. Focus is on attitude and personality scales rather than single attitude items. Chapters address life satisfaction and happiness, self-esteem, social anxiety, depression and loneliness, alienation, locus of control, authoritarianism, androgyny and general measures of value.

Spreen, Otfried, and Esther Strauss. *A Compendium of Neuropsychological Tests: Administration, Norms, and Commentary*. 2nd ed. New York : Oxford University Press, 1998.
This compendium describes approximately 80 tests in eight broad categories: cognitive, achievement, attention/memory, language, visual/auditory, tactile, motor, and adaptive behavior/personality. Indexed by name, test title, and subject.

"Statement on the use of secure psychological tests in the education of graduate and undergraduate psychology students" (American Psychological Association Science Directorate) http://www.apa.org/science/securetests.html
Developed by the Committee on Psychological Tests and Assessment (CPTA), this statement addresses the issue of test security for the teaching and training purposes of students in psychology.

Suzuki, Lisa A., Joseph G. Ponterotto, and Paul J. Meller. *The New Handbook of Multicultural Assessment: Clinical, Psychological, and Educational Applications*. 2nd ed. San Francisco, Calif.: Jossey-Bass, 2000.
This handbook covers research, issues, and methods in multicultural assessment, including major instruments and procedures, cognitive and educational assessment, cross-cultural sensitivity and ethics, as well as emerging issues in the field. Contributions are provided from experts in the fields of psychometrics, assessment, and evaluation.

Test Critiques. Kansas City, Mo.: Test Corporation of America, c.1984–1990.
Austin, Tex.: Pro-Ed, 1991– .
Easy to use, comprehensive resource providing descriptive information, critiques and references on the major recommended psychological, educational and business tests. Beginning with v. 3, each volume has included an updated cumulative subject index.

Tests in Microfiche. Princeton, N.J.: Educational Testing Service, 1975– .
This annual series of unpublished research instruments that have been cited in the educational and psychological literature includes areas such as self-concept, attitudes, and personality traits. Each set contains instruments designed for different populations, and is accompanied by an annotated index. It is searchable online using the ERIC/AE Test Locator (see ERIC above).

Tests in Print. Lincoln, Neb.: Buros Institute of Mental Measurements, University of Nebraska-Lincoln, 1961– .
Each of these irregularly published volumes serves as both a cumulative index to the *Mental Measurements Yearbooks* (*MMY*) series, and a comprehensive bibliography of every commercially available test in print at the time of publication. Like the *MMY*, *TIP* includes indexes of titles, acronyms, names, and scores, a directory and index to publishers, and a classified subject index. *TIP* also provides an index of tests that have gone out of print since the last edition. See also: *Mental Measurements Yearbook.*

Touliatos, John, Barry F. Perlmutter, and Murray A. Straus. *Handbook of Family Measurement Techniques.* Newbury Park, Calif.: Sage, 1990.
This handbook lists, with abstracts, nearly 1000 instruments associated with family-related issues. Over 500 of those presented have been cited in published literature since 1975. Entries for instruments, grouped in five general categories, contain abstracts and provide information about content and procedures for using each test.

U.S. Department of Labor. Employment and Training Administration. Office of Policy and Research. "Testing and Assessment: An Employer's Guide to Good Practices."
http://www.doleta.gov/opr/FULLTEXT/99-testassess.pdf
This site provides managers and human resource professionals with guidance in using assessment practices that will best meet the needs of their organizations. Easily understood terms are used, and the complete document is available for downloading in pdf file format.

U.S. Department of Labor. Employment and Training Administration. Office of Policy and Research. "Tests and other assessments: helping you make better career decisions."
http://www.doleta.gov/opr/fulltext/00-testother.pdf
Directed to the test-taker, this site describes the different types of career assessment tools, and how they might guide an individual in making a career choice. The complete document is available for downloading in pdf file format.

Zalaquett, Carlos P. and Richard J. Wood. *Evaluating Stress: A Book of Resources.* Lanham, Md. Scarecrow Press, 1997.
Covers 21 different instruments for the evaluation of stress or stress-related factors, with information on each presented by its original author. Criteria for inclusion in this volume were having the instrument published or listed in well-known test review sources, ERIC, and PsycLIT. Each chapter includes examples of how the instrument can be applied and where it may be obtained.

Zeliff, Nancy and Kimberly Schultz. *Authentic Assessment in Action: Preparing for the Business Workplace.* Little Rock, Ark.: Delta Pi Epsilon, 1998.
Following the content areas designated in the National Standards for Business Education, this guide discusses the types of tests and inventories used in schools and the workplace. It includes a glossary of terms, bibliography, and examples of assessment instruments.

Bibliography

Ash, Lee, and William G. Miller. *Subject Collections: A Guide to Special Book Collections and Subject Emphases as Reported by University, College, Public, and Special Libraries and Museums in the United States and Canada.* 7th ed. New Providence, N.J.: R.R. Bowker, 1993.

The College Blue Book. 26th ed. New York: Macmillan, 1997.

Directory of Curriculum Materials Centers. 4th ed. Chicago: Association of College and Research Libraries, American Library Association, 1996.

Fabiano, Emily, and Nancy O'Brien. *Testing Information Sources for Educators.* (ERIC/ TME report ; 94). Princeton, N.J.: ERIC Clearinghouse on Tests, Measurement, and Evaluation, Educational Testing Service, 1987.

Ginn, David, and Nancy O'Brien. "Selected Test Collections in the United States: A Survey of Organization." *Behavioral & Social Sciences Librarian* 4 (2/3): 9–20, 1985.

Grossman, Cheryl R. Sturko. "A Survey of the Organization and Management of Current and Historical Test Collections." *Behavioral & Social Sciences Librarian* 17 (2): 11–32, 1999.

Guide for the Development and Management of Test Collections: With Special Emphasis on Academic Settings. Chicago: American Library Association, 1985.

McGiverin, Rolland H. *Educational and Psychological Tests in the Academic Library.* New York: Haworth Press, 1990.

Piotrowski, Chris, and Bob Perdue. "Reference Sources on Psychological Tests: A Contemporary Review." *Behavioral & Social Sciences Librarian* 17 (2): 47–58, 1999.

Wygant, Ted M. "Use Pattern Analysis of a Test Collection." *Behavioral & Social Sciences Librarian.* 15 (2): 1–20, 1997.

Azusa Pacific University
Hugh & Hazel Darling Library and William V. Marshburn Library
901 E. Alosta Ave.
P.O. Box 7000
Azusa, California 91702

Contact Person(s): Debra Quast, David Holifield
E-mail address: dquast@apu.edu, dholifield@apu.edu
Telephone: 626-815-6000 ext.5066
Fax number: 626-815-5064
Library/Collection Internet address(es):
  http://www.apu.edu
  http://www.apu.edu/library/onlineResources.html

Collection Access/Use

Tests may be used by: institutional faculty, graduate students, undergraduate students.

Tests are available for: check-out to faculty/students, check-out with written approval.

Loan period: 2 weeks.

Collection Data

Size (titles and/or editions): between 501-1000.

Strengths:

Achievement
Aptitude
Behavior Assessment
Developmental
Education

Intelligence and Scholastic Aptitude
Multi-Aptitude Batteries
Personality
Reading
Vocations

General Information: ETS Tests in Microfiche, Sets A-Y and ERIC documents.

Various test kits available to students enrolled in specific courses (faculty signature is required for student checkout). Additional tests available in Psy.D. and Ed.D. departments via vertical files.

Historical components/elements?: None Reported.

California

California Polytechnic State University - San Luis Obispo
Robert E. Kennedy Library
San Luis Obispo, California 93407

Contact Person(s): Mary Louise Brady
E-mail address: mbrady@calpoly.edu
Telephone: 805-756-2273
Fax number: 805-756-2346
Library/Collection Internet address(es):
 http://www.lib.calpoly.edu

Collection Access/Use

Tests may be used by: institutional faculty, graduate students, undergraduate students, outside professionals.

Tests are available for: check-out to faculty/students (faculty without written approval), check-out with written approval (students).

Loan period: 2 days.

Collection Data

Size (titles and/or editions): between 501-1000.

Strengths:

Achievement
Aptitude
Behavior Assessment
Education
Intelligence and Scholastic Aptitude
Multi-Aptitude Batteries

Neuropsychological
Personality
Reading
Speech & Hearing
Vocations

General Information: The main purpose of the collection is to provide study material for our education students. 95% of our tests are specimen sets. We have the ETS Tests in Microfiche Collection Sets A-X.

Historical Components/elements?: None Reported.

California School of Professional Psychology - Fresno
Library (Circulation Desk)
5130 East Clinton Way
Fresno, California 93727

Contact Person(s): Louise Colbert, MLS
E-mail address: lcolbert@mail.cspp.edu
Telephone: 559-253-2265 ext.2252
Fax number: 559-253-2223

Collection Access/Use

Tests may be used by: institutional faculty, graduate students.

Tests are available for: in-house use only, check-out to faculty/students.

Loan period: 2 days.

Collection Data

Size (titles and/or editions): between 100 and 500.

Strengths:

Achievement
Aptitude
Behavior Assessment
Developmental

Neuropsychological
Personality
Speech & Hearing

General Information: Our test collections are not available for check out by non-CSPP persons. We purchase them for educational purposes only and are rather restrictive in allowing their use.

Historical components/elements?: Yes, we preserve 1-2 archival copies of most tests which are superseded by newer editions and revisions.

California

California School of Professional Psychology, Los Angeles Campus
Library
1000 S. Fremont Ave.
Alhambra, California 91001

Contact Person(s): Public Services Librarian
Telephone: 626-284-2777 ext. 3460
Fax number: 626-284-1682

Collection Access/Use

Tests may be used by: institutional faculty, graduate students.

Tests are available for: in-house use only, check-out to faculty/students, check-out with written approval.

Loan period: varies from 2 hours to two weeks.

Collection Data

Size (titles and/or editions): between 100 and 500.

Strengths:

Behavior Assessment
Developmental
Neuropsychological

Personality
Sensory Motor

General Information: Continuing subscription to ETS Tests in Microfiche, beginning with Set A.

The CSPP-LA Test Collection is a heavily used clinical collection, acquired and managed to support graduate clinical psychology students in assessment courses and internships.

Access is limited to CSPP students and faculty.

Historical components/elements?: None Reported.

California State University - Chico
Meriam Library
Curriculum Department
Chico, California 95929-0295

Contact Person(s): Marcia McAndress, Library Assistant III, Supervisor/Manager
E-mail address: mmcandress@csuchico.edu
Telephone: 530-898-5266
Library/Collection Internet address(es):
   http://www.csuchico.edu/library/index.html

Collection Access/Use

Tests may be used by: institutional faculty, graduate students, undergraduate students.

Tests are available for: check-out with written approval.

Loan period: 1-3 days.

Collection Data

Size (titles and/or editions): between 100 and 500 (limited loan tests).

Strengths:

Achievement
Aptitude
Behavior Assessment
Developmental
Education
English
Fine Arts
Foreign Languages
Intelligence and Scholastic Aptitude
Mathematics

Miscellaneous
Multi-Aptitude Batteries
Neuropsychological
Personality
Reading
Sensory Motor
Social Studies
Speech & Hearing
Vocations

General Information: We have not been updating our collection of tests for many years. We have a small staff and a large curriculum K-12 collection that is our major focus. We do, however, receive and catalog some standardized tests to accompany textbooks.

Historical components/elements?: Yes, our collection is old, but does not qualify as "historical". We no longer update except for tests that may accompany K-12 textbooks.

California

California State University - Fullerton
Paulina June & George Pollak Library
P.O. Box 4150
Fullerton, California 92834-4150

Contact Person(s): Mary Crimmins, Coordinator, Audiovisual & Curriculum Materials Center
E-mail address: mcrimmins@fullerton.edu
Telephone: 714-278-2151
Library/Collection Internet address(es):
   http://www.library.fullerton.edu

Collection Access/Use

> **Tests may be used by:** institutional faculty, graduate students, undergraduate students, outside professionals.

> **Tests are available for:** in-house use only, check-out to faculty/students, check-out with written approval (use of some tests is restricted to two hour in-house use only to students whose names appear on a class list).

> **Loan period:** Some educational tests circulate for 2 days, others for two weeks.

Collection Data

Size (titles and/or editions): between 100 and 500.

General Information: This is a closed, paged collection exclusively for the use of students and faculty enrolled in relevant courses at California State University, Fullerton. Items from the Test Collection may not be borrowed on interlibrary loan, and many can be used only by designated students and faculty.

Historical components/elements?: Our collection does include old and out-of-date tests.

California State University - Long Beach
University Library
1250 Bellflower Blvd.
Long Beach, California 90840-1901

Contact Person(s): Tiffini Travis
E-mail address: ttravis@csulb.edu
Telephone: 562-985-7850
Fax number: 562-985-1703

Collection Access/Use

Tests may be used by: institutional faculty, graduate students, undergraduate students, outside professionals, general public.

Tests are available for: in-house use only.

Collection Data

Size (titles and/or editions): between 500 and 1000.

Strengths:

Aptitude
Behavior Assessment
Education
English

Mathematics
Miscellaneous
Personality
Reading

General Information: ETS Tests in Microfiche, Sets A-Q (1975-1991).

Historical components/elements?: Yes, Dates covered: 1975-1991.

Colorado

University of Northern Colorado
Library
Greeley, Colorado 80639

Contact Person(s): Jan Squire
E-mail address: jsquire@unco.edu
Telephone: 970-351-1521
Fax number: 970-351-2540
Library/Collection Internet address(es):
  http://source.unco.edu

Collection Access/Use

Tests may be used by: institutional faculty, graduate students, undergraduate students, outside professionals, general public.

Tests are available for: in-house use only, check-out to faculty/students, check-out with written approval, check-out to outside researchers.

Loan period: 4 weeks undergraduate, 8 weeks graduate.

Collection Data

Size (titles and/or editions): between 1000 and 2000.

Strengths:

Achievement
Aptitude
Behavior Assessment
Developmental
Education

Multi-Aptitude Batteries
Neuropsychological
Personality
Reading
Speech & Hearing

Historical Components/elements?: None Reported.

University of Southern Colorado
Library
2200 Bonforte Blvd.
Pueblo, Colorado 81001

Contact Person(s): Ann Kuntzman, Reference Librarian
E-mail address: kuntzman@uscolo.edu
Telephone: 719-549-2432
Fax number: 719-549-2738
Library/Collection Internet address(es):
    http://www.uscolo.edu/library

Collection Access/Use

Tests may be used by: institutional faculty, graduate students, undergraduate students, outside professionals, general public.

Tests are available for: in-house use only.

Collection Data

Size (titles and/or editions): between 100 and 500.

General Information: Have Mental Measurements Yearbooks, 1959, 1965, 1972, 1978, 1985, 1989, 1992, 1995, 1998.

No tests other than GRE, GMAT, LSAT1, TESOL guides.

Historical components/elements?: Yes.

Delaware

University of Delaware
Education Resource Center
012 Willard Hall Education Bldg.
Newark, Delaware 19716-2940

Contact Person(s): Beth G. Anderson
E-mail address: edubeth@udel.edu
Telephone: 302-831-6308
Fax number: 302-831-8404
Library/Collection Internet address(es):
    http://www.udel.edu/erc

Collection Access/Use

Tests may be used by: institutional faculty, graduate students, undergraduate students, outside professionals, general public.

Tests are available for: in-house use only, check-out to faculty/students, check-out with written approval.

Loan period: 3 days.

Collection Data

Size (titles and/or editions): between 100 and 500.

Strengths:

Achievement	Developmental
Aptitude	Intelligence and Scholastic Aptitude
Behavior Assessment	Personality

General Information: We have approximately 100 ETS Tests in Microfiche, but have not determined what set or sets they may represent.

We supply consumable answer sheets at no cost to undergraduate and graduate students who are required to administer tests.

Historical components/elements?: Yes, approximately 200 titles from the 1970s have been retained.

Florida International University
Green Library, Curriculum Collection
University Park Campus
Miami, Florida 33199

Contact Person(s): Dr. H. Minnie Dunbar
E-mail address: dunbarm@fiu.edu
Telephone: 305-348-2415
Fax number: 305-348-3408
Library/Collection Internet address(es):
    http://www.fiu.edu/~library/assistance/uptests.html

Collection Access/Use

Tests may be used by: institutional faculty graduate students, undergraduate students, outside professionals, general public.

Tests are available for: in-house use only.

Collection Data

Size (titles and/or editions): <100.

Strengths:

Achievement
Aptitude
Education
English
Mathematics
Multi-Aptitude Batteries

Personality
Reading
Sensory Motor
Social Studies
Speech & Hearing

Historical Components/elements?: None Reported.

Georgia

Georgia School of Professional Psychology
Library
990 Hammond Drive NE
Atlanta, Georgia 30328

Contact Person(s): David McCullough
E-mail address: dmccullo@gspp.edu
Telephone: 770-671-1200
Fax number: 770-671-0418

Collection Access/Use

Tests may be used by: institutional faculty, graduate students.

Tests are available for: in-house use only, check-out to faculty/students.

Loan period: variable.

Collection Data

Size (titles and/or editions): between 100 and 500.

Strengths:

Achievement
Aptitude
Behavior Assessment
Multi-Aptitude Batteries

Neuropsychological
Personality
Sensory Motor

General Information: Tests are solely for the use of current students and faculty for course work and, to the extent course work doesn't monopolize the tests, for practice.

Historical Components/elements?: None Reported.

Chicago School of Professional Psychology
Library
47 West Polk St., 2nd Floor
Chicago, Illinois 60605

Contact Person(s): Margaret White
E-mail address: PWhite@csopp.edu
Telephone: 312-786-9443 ext.3002
Fax number: 312-786-9611
Library/Collection Internet address(es):
   www.csopp.edu/links.html

Collection Access/Use

Tests may be used by: institutional faculty, graduate students, outside professionals.

Tests are available for: in-house use only, check-out to faculty/students.

Loan period: Usually overnight, but can vary according to circumstance/need.

Collection Data

Size (titles and/or editions): between 100 and 500.

Strengths:

Achievement
Aptitude
Behavior Assessment
Developmental

Intelligence and Scholastic Aptitude
Neuropsychological
Personality
Sensory Motor

Historical components/elements?: Yes, our collection contains previous editions of a number of tests.

Illinois

Chicago State University
Curriculum Materials Center, 334 Douglas Library
9501 S. King Ave.
Chicago, Illinois 60628

Contact Person(s): Beverly Meyer
E-mail address: B-Meyer@csu.edu
Telephone: 773-995-2587
Fax number: 773-995-3772
Library/Collection Internet address(es):
   http://www.csu.edu/library/

Collection Access/Use

Tests may be used by: institutional faculty, graduate students, undergraduate students, outside professionals, general public.

Tests are available for: in-house use only.

Collection Data

Size (titles and/or editions): between 100 and 500.

Strengths:

Achievement   Reading
Aptitude

Historical components/elements?: Yes, we have copies of some pretty old tests!

Concordia University (Illinois)
Library
7400 Augusta Street
River Forest, Illinois 60305

Contact Person(s): Barb Peterson
E-mail address: crfPetersbl@curf.edu; crflibrary@curf.edu
Telephone: 708-209-3055
Fax number: 708-209-3531

Collection Access/Use

Tests may be used by: institutional faculty under specific conditions, graduate students under specific conditions, undergraduate students under specific conditions.

Tests are available for: check-out with written approval.

Loan period: 1 week with approval.

Collection Data

Size (titles and/or editions): between 100 and 500.

Strengths:

Achievement
Aptitude
Behavior Assessment
Developmental

Miscellaneous
Multi-Aptitude Batteries
Personality

General Information: Closed collection -- usable only by specific classes.

Historical Components/elements?: None Reported.

Illinois

Illinois State University
Milner Library/Education and Psychology Division
Campus Box 8900
Normal, Illinois 61790-8900

Contact Person(s): James Huff, Psychology Reference Librarian
E-mail address: james@exchange1.mlb.ilstu.edu
Telephone: 309-438-3441
Fax number: 309-438-3676
Library/Collection Internet address(es):
> http://www.mlb.ilstu.edu

Collection Access/Use

> **Tests may be used by:** institutional faculty, graduate students, undergraduate students, outside professionals, general public.

> **Tests are available for:** in-house use only (by policy, tests are only available for examination in the library); check-out with written approval (On very rare occasions, an exception may be made to allow check-out for a short time, such as a graduate student doing a presentation for a class. The tests are intended for educational use, and not for professional administration).

Collection Data

Size (titles and/or editions): between 501-1000.

Strengths:

Achievement	Miscellaneous
Aptitude	Neuropsychological
Developmental	Speech & Hearing
Education	

General Information: By policy, this collection does not contain restricted tests (tests whose use is restricted to appropriate professionals), usually defined as intelligence tests, projective tests, adult personality tests, and adult vocational tests. The university psychology department maintains these types of tests separately for use in training their students, and for research.

The above information applies to the test collection that Milner Library has assembled. We also have ETS Tests in Microfiche.

Historical components/elements?: No, this is intended as a current awareness collection only.

Southern Illinois University at Carbondale
Instructional Materials Center, Education and Psychology Division
6632 Morris Library
555 W. Grand
Carbondale, Illinois 62901

Contact Person(s): Roland Person
E-mail address: rperson@lib.siu.edu
Telephone: 618-453-1651
Fax number: 618-453-2704
Library/Collection Internet address(es):
   http://www.lib.siu.edu

<u>Collection Access/Use</u>

Tests may be used by: institutional faculty, graduate students, undergraduate students, outside professionals, general public.

Tests are available for: in-house use only.

<u>Collection Data</u>

Size (titles and/or editions): between 1000 and 2000.

Strengths:

Achievement   Personality
Intelligence and Scholastic Aptitude

General Information: ETS Tests in Microfiche, Sets A-M. In general, tests are in locked files and do not circulate, but are available to users anytime this division of the library is open.

Historical components/elements?: Yes, as each new MMY or TIP appears, those tests no longer listed as being in print are removed from the "Tests in Print" cabinet and placed in the "Historical" cabinet.

Illinois

University of Illinois at Chicago
Curriculum
P.O.Box 8198, M/C 234
Chicago, Illinois 60680

Contact Person(s): Joan B Fiscella, Bibliographer; Mary Losew, Supervisor of Curriculum Library
E-mail address: jbf@uic.edu
Telephone: 312-996-2730
Fax number: 312-413-0424
Library/Collection Internet address(es):
> http://www.uic.edu/depts/lib/
> http://www.uic.edu/depts/lib/sysdoc/uiccat
> (On that page you have a choice between a web interface and a telnet interface.)

Collection Access/Use
> **Tests may be used by:** institutional faculty, graduate students, undergraduate students, outside professionals, general public.
>
> **Tests are available for:** in-house use only, limited photocopy to students required to administer test. Faculty member makes arrangements and identifies eligible students.

Collection Data

Size (titles and/or editions): between 1000 and 2000.

Strengths:

Achievement
Aptitude
Developmental
English
Mathematics

Miscellaneous
Personality
Reading
Vocations

General Information: ETS Tests in Microfiche. Since UIC is a public university, anyone may come in to use the test collection. Only manuals and technical reports can be photocopied (except as noted above).

Historical Components/elements?: None Reported.

University of Illinois at Urbana-Champaign
Education and Social Science Library
100 Main Library
1408 Gregory Dr.
Urbana, Illinois 61801

Contact Person(s): Nancy P. O'Brien
E-mail address: n-obrien@uiuc.edu (Ask-A-Librarian educlib@uiuc.edu)
Telephone: 217-333-2305
Fax number: 217-333-2214
Library/Collection Internet address(es):
> http://www.library.uiuc.edu/edx/
> http://www.library.uiuc.edu/edx/testcoll/input.asp

Collection Access/Use

Tests may be used by: institutional faculty, graduate students, undergraduate students, outside professionals, general public.

Tests are available for: in-house use only (Materials may not be checked out).

Collection Data

Size (titles and/or editions): 2000 or more.

Strengths:

Achievement	Mathematics
Aptitude	Miscellaneous
Behavior Assessment	Multi-Aptitude Batteries
Education	Personality
English	Reading
Foreign Languages	Social Studies
Intelligence and Scholastic Aptitude	Vocations

General Information: The test collection of the Education and Social Science Library contains over 8,000 tests measuring achievement, intelligence, character and personality, vocational aptitude and many other subjects. Tests dating from 1914 to the present are included and are classified according to the system used by Buros in the earlier Mental Measurement Yearbooks. A list of the test classifications is available.

Test packets usually contain a copy of the test form, a manual and a scoring key.

Illinois

The Education and Social Science Library also owns a collection of tests on microfiche. This collection provides access to unpublished tests. ETS Tests in Microfiche, Annotated Index, (Sets A-X) indexes these tests by title, subject and author and is available on site.

Test packets do not leave the library and copying is prohibited.

See http://www.library.uiuc.edu/edx/tests.htm for further information.

Historical components/elements?: Yes, tests dating from 1914 to the present are included and are classified according to the system used by Buros in the earlier Mental Measurement Yearbooks.

Indiana State University
Library
Teaching Materials, Microforms and Media Dept.
Terre Haute, Indiana 47809

Contact Person(s): Rolland H. McGiverin
E-mail address: libgilb@cml.indstate.edu
Telephone: 812-237-2617
Fax number: 812-237-2567
Library/Collection Internet address(es):
   http://odin.indstate.edu

Collection Access/Use

Tests may be used by: institutional faculty, graduate students, undergraduate students, outside professionals.

Tests are available for: in-house use only, check-out with written approval.

Loan period: 2 hours (in-house). Other loan periods determined by dept. head.

Collection Data

Size (titles and/or editions): between 501-1000.

General Information: ETS Tests in Microfiche (Sets A-P). No restrictions on the [microfiche] collection.

Historical Components/elements?: None Reported.

Iowa

American College Testing
ACT Library
2201 N. Dodge Street
Iowa City, Iowa 52243-0168

Contact Person(s): Jacqueline Snider, Library Manager
E-mail address: snider@act.org
Telephone: 319-337-1166
Fax number: 319-339-3021

Collection Access/Use

Tests may be used by: institutional faculty, staff.

Tests are available for: check-out to faculty/students (kept in locked cabinet,; checked out for brief periods of time).

Loan period: one month.

Collection Data

Size (titles and/or editions): between 501-1000.

Strengths:

Achievement
Aptitude
Education
English

Intelligence and Scholastic Aptitude
Mathematics
Multi-Aptitude Batteries
Vocations

General Information: We circulate tests only to ACT staff.

Historical Components/elements?: None Reported.

University of Iowa
Blommers Measurement Resources Library
Iowa Testing Programs (College of Education)
304 Lindquist Center
Iowa City, Iowa 52402

Contact Person(s): Martha R. Wilding
E-mail address: martha-wilding@uiowa.edu
Telephone: 319-335-5416
Fax number: 319-335-6038

Collection Access/Use

Tests may be used by: institutional faculty, graduate students. undergraduate students, outside professionals, general public.

Tests are available for: check-out to faculty/students, check-out to outside researchers (under certain circumstances).

Loan period: 1 week.

Collection Data

Size (titles and/or editions): 2000 or more (current and historical tests).

Strengths:

Achievement
Aptitude
Education
Multi-Aptitude Batteries

Neuropsychological
Personality
NOTE: Collection includes some tests in all categories.

General Information: We have three parts to our test collection: Current tests (1000), ETS Tests in Microfiche (all sets); and Historical Tests. Our collection also includes approx. 5000 books and reports on the subjects of measurement and statistics.

Historical components/elements?: Yes, large collection of out-of-print tests/superseded editions dating back to the early 1900s. Not sure of number of tests in this file.

Iowa

University of Northern Iowa
Instructional Resources and Technology Services, College of Education
222 Schindler Education Center
Cedar Falls, Iowa 50614-0609

Contact Person(s): Matthew Kollasch, Director or Maxine Davis, Co-ordinator
E-mail address: Matthew.Kollasch@uni.edu or Maxine.Davis@uni.edu
Telephone: 319-273-6066
Fax number: 319-273-6997
Library/Collection Internet address(es):
   http://unistar.uni.edu

Collection Access/Use

Tests may be used by: institutional faculty, graduate students, undergraduate students, outside professionals, general public.

Tests are available for: in-house use only, check-out to faculty/students, check-out to outside researchers.

Loan period: 1 week.

Collection Data

Size (titles and/or editions): between 100 and 500.

Strengths:

Achievement
Aptitude
Behavior Assessment
Developmental
Education
English
Fine Arts
Intelligence and Scholastic Aptitude
Mathematics

Multi-Aptitude Batteries
Personality
Reading
Sensory Motor
Social Studies
Speech & Hearing
Vocations
Science, Health, Physical Education, and Home Economics

Historical components/elements?: Yes.

Washburn University of Topeka
Mabee Library, Curriculum Resources Center
1700 SW College Ave.
Topeka, Kansas 66621

Contact Person(s): Judy Druse
E-mail address: crclbrn@washburn.edu
Telephone: 785-231-1010 ext.1277
Fax number: 785-357-1240
Library/Collection Internet address(es):
> http://www.washburn.edu/mabee/crc.htm
> http://lib.wuacc.edu

Collection Access/Use

> **Tests may be used by:** institutional faculty, graduate students, undergraduate students, outside professionals, general public.

> **Tests are available for:** in-house use only, check-out to faculty/students, check-out with written approval, check-out to outside researchers.

> **Loan period:** 3 weeks.

Collection Data

Size (titles and/or editions): between 100 and 500.

Strengths:

Achievement	Education
Aptitude	Multi-Aptitude Batteries
Behavior Assessment	Reading
Developmental	Sensory Motor

Historical Components/elements?: None Reported.

Kentucky

Spalding University
Library
853 Library Lane
Louisville, Kentucky 40203

Contact Person(s): Jan Poston
E-mail address: spaldlib@iglou.com
Telephone: 502-585-7130
Fax number: 502-585-7156
Library/Collection Internet address(es):
   http://www.spalding.edu/library/index.html

Collection Access/Use

Tests may be used by: institutional faculty, graduate students, undergraduate students.

Tests are available for: in-house use only, check-out to faculty/students.

Loan period: 5 days.

Collection Data

Size (titles and/or editions): between 100 and 500.

Strengths:

Achievement
Aptitude
Behavior Assessment
Multi-Aptitude Batteries

Neuropsychological
Personality
Reading
Sensory Motor

General Information: Our collection is very heavily used by our psychology faculty and graduate students so we cannot loan items through interlibrary loan. Please contact us for on-site viewing.

Historical Components/elements?: None Reported.

Boston College
Campion Hall
140 Commonwealth Avenue
Chestnut Hill, Massachusetts 02467

Contact Person(s): Monique Lowd
E-mail address: lowd@bc.edu
Telephone: 617-552-4919
Fax number: 617-552-1769
Library/Collection Internet address(es):
   http://www.bc.edu/bc_org/avp/ulib/bclib.html

Collection Access/Use

Tests may be used by: institutional faculty assuming test is unrestricted, graduate students assuming test is unrestricted, undergraduate students assuming test is unrestricted, outside professionals assuming test is unrestricted, general public assuming test is unrestricted.

Tests are available for: in-house use only, check-out to faculty/students.

Loan period: 3 days.

Collection Data

Size (titles and/or editions): between 100 and 500.

Strengths:

Aptitude	Mathematics
Developmental	Neuropsychological
Education	Sensory Motor
Intelligence and Scholastic Aptitude	Speech & Hearing

General Information: The main library subscribes to ETS Tests in Microfiche

Historical Components/elements?: None Reported.

Massachusetts

Bridgewater State College
Curriculum Library/Clement C. Maxwell Library
Bridgewater, Massachusetts 02325

Contact Person(s): Robert M. Simmons
E-mail address: rsimmons@bridgew.edu, curlib@bridgew.edu
Telephone: 508-697-1304
Library/Collection Internet address(es):
    http://www.bridgew.edu/depts/maxwell/currlib.htm

Collection Access/Use

Tests may be used by: institutional faculty, graduate students, undergraduate students, outside professionals, general public (if they meet certain qualifications).

Tests are available for: in-house use only, we sometimes let them out by special permission.

Loan period: special permissions for class period only.

Collection Data

Size (titles and/or editions): between 501-1000.

Strengths:

Achievement
Aptitude
Behavior Assessment
Developmental

Education
Intelligence and Scholastic Aptitude
Reading
Speech & Hearing

General Information: We have ETS Tests in Microfiche in addition to our standardized test collection. Our test use policy is included on our Web page.

Historical Components/elements?: None Reported.

Harvard Graduate School of Education
Monroe C. Gutman Library
6 Appian Way
Cambridge, Massachusetts 02138

Contact Person(s): Gladys I. Dratch
E-mail address: gladys_dratch@harvard.edu
Telephone: 617-496-3108
Fax number: 617-495-0540
Library/Collection Internet address(es):
> http://gseweb.harvard.edu/~library
> http://hplus.harvard.edu

Collection Access/Use

> **Tests may be used by:** institutional faculty, graduate students, undergraduate students, outside professionals, general public.

> **Tests are available for:** in-house use only.

> **Loan period:** 2 hour, in-house use.

Collection Data

Size (titles and/or editions): 2000 or more.

Strengths:

Achievement
Aptitude
Behavior Assessment
Developmental
Education
English
Intelligence and Scholastic Aptitude
Mathematics

Multi-Aptitude Batteries
Neuropsychological
Personality
Reading
Sensory Motor
Social Studies
Vocations

General Information: Library use only. Tests may not be administered. Holdings include the ETS Tests in Microfiche, sets A-X.

Historical components/elements?: Yes, a large portion of the collection consists of older tests (pre-1970). Current purchases support the Graduate School of Education course work on testing.

Massachusetts

Salem State College
Education Resource Library
352 Lafayette St.
Salem, Massachusetts 01970

Contact Person(s): Barbara E. Husbands, Assistant Librarian
E-mail address: bhusband@salem.mass.edu
Telephone: 978-542-6967
Fax number: 978-744-6596
Library/Collection Internet address(es):
> http://www.salem.mass.edu/library/index.htm

Collection Access/Use

Tests may be used by: institutional faculty, graduate students, undergraduate students.

Tests are available for: check-out with written approval.

Loan period: 1 week.

Collection Data

Size (titles and/or editions): between 100 and 500.

Strengths:

Achievement
Aptitude
Behavior Assessment
Developmental

Multi-Aptitude Batteries
Personality
Reading
Sensory Motor

Historical Components/elements?: None Reported.

Massachusetts

University of Massachusetts - Boston
Curriculum Library/Joseph P. Healey Library
100 Morrissey Blvd.
Boston, Massachusetts 02125-3393

Contact Person(s): Verna B. Okali
E-mail address: verna@delphinus.lib.umb.edu
Telephone: 617-287-5945
Fax number: 617-287-5950
Library/Collection Internet address(es):
   http://www.lib.umb.edu

Collection Access/Use

Tests may be used by: institutional faculty, graduate students, outside professionals, consortium members.

Tests are available for: in-house use only, check-out to faculty/students, check-out with written approval.

Loan period: 24 hours (overnight).

Collection Data

Size (titles and/or editions): between 100 and 500.

Strengths:

Achievement
Aptitude
Developmental
Education
English
Foreign Languages
Intelligence and Scholastic Aptitude
Mathematics

Personality
Reading
Sensory Motor
Social Studies
Speech & Hearing
Vocations
Bilingual education/second language acquisition

Historical Components/elements?: None Reported.

Massachusetts

Westfield State College
Education Resources Center/Ely Library
Western Avenue
Westfield, Massachusetts 01086-1630

Contact Person(s): Dr. Signia Warner
E-mail address: s_warner@foma.wsc.edu
Telephone: 413-572-5235 (ERC)
Fax number: 413-572-5520 (Ely Library fax)
Library/Collection Internet address(es):
    htttp://bondo.wsc.mass.edu/dept/dept/library/library.htm

Collection Access/Use

Tests may be used by: institutional faculty, graduate students, undergraduate students.

Tests are available for: check-out with written approval.

Loan period: 1 week (in-house only with permission of instructor).

Collection Data

Size (titles and/or editions): between 100 and 500.

Strengths:

Achievement
Aptitude
Behavior Assessment
Developmental

Education
Mathematics
Multi-Aptitude Batteries
Reading

Historical Components/elements?: None Reported.

Worcester State College
Library
486 Chandler Street
Worcester, Massachusetts 01602-2597

Contact Person(s): Donald Hochstetler
E-mail address: dhochstetler@worcester.edu
Telephone: 508-929-8511
Fax number: 508-929-8198
Library/Collection Internet address(es):
    http://www.worcester.edu/library

Collection Access/Use

Tests may be used by: institutional faculty, graduate students, undergraduate students, outside professionals, general public.

Tests are available for: in-house use only.

Collection Data

Size (titles and/or editions): between 100 and 500.

Strengths:

Achievement
Aptitude
Behavior Assessment
Developmental
Education
English
Fine Arts
Mathematics

Multi-Aptitude Batteries
Neuropsychological
Personality
Reading
Sensory Motor
Social Studies
Speech & Hearing
Vocations

Historical Components/elements?: None Reported.

Michigan

University of Michigan
School of Education
2007 School of Education
610 East University Street
Ann Arbor, Michigan 48109-1259

Contact Person(s): Donna Estabrook
E-mail address: destabro@umich.edu
Telephone: 734-647-2418
Fax number: 734-647-2218
Library/Collection Internet address(es):
    http://www.soe.umich.edu/resources/techserv/iris.html#aboutext

Collection Access/Use

Tests may be used by: institutional faculty, graduate students (with faculty permission).

Tests are available for: check-out to faculty/students (graduate students with faculty approval), check-out with written approval.

Loan period: negotiated loan period.

Collection Data

Size (titles and/or editions): between 1000 and 2000.

Strengths:

Developmental
Education
Intelligence and Scholastic Aptitude

Reading
Sensory Motor

General Information: We have only a few tests specifically requested by faculty and not regularly updated. Since they are available to faculty only, they are not even mentioned on our web site.

Historical components/elements?: Yes, we have some older editions of Stanford-Binet (1972).

Wayne State University
Purdy/Kresge Library
5265 Cass Ave.
Detroit, Michigan 48202

Contact Person(s): Shellie Jeffries
E-mail address: ac0656@wayne.edu
Telephone: 313-577-4217
Fax number: 313-577-3436
Library/Collection Internet address(es):
    http://www.lib.wayne/edu/purdy

Collection Access/Use

Tests may be used by: institutional faculty, graduate students, undergraduate students, outside professionals, general public.

Tests are available for: in-house use only.

Collection Data

Size (titles and/or editions): between 100 and 500.

Strengths:

Achievement	Mathematics
Aptitude	Personality
English	Reading
Intelligence and Scholastic Aptitude	Vocations

General Information: We do have ETS Tests in Microfiche, Sets A-X and anticipate continuing to subscribe to this ETS service.

Historical components/elements?: Yes, you might say that our print test collection is nearly completely historical. It contains about 450 tests published between 1920 and 1986; 81% of these tests were published between 1920 and 1959. The remaining 19% were published at a later date and only seven of them date from the 1980s. We are not currently adding to the collection. All print tests are located at our Reserve Desk.

Minnesota

Concordia University (Minnesota)
Buenger Memorial Library
275 Syndicate Street North
St. Paul, Minnesota 55104-5494

Contact Person(s): Martha Burkart
E-mail address: mburkart@luther.csp.edu
Telephone: 651-641-8242
Fax number: 651-659-0207
Library/Collection Internet address(es):
    http://www.csp.edu/VirtualLibrary/

Collection Access/Use

Tests may be used by: institutional faculty, graduate students, undergraduate students, outside professionals, general public.

Tests are available for: check-out to faculty/students.

Loan period: 3 days.

Collection Data

Size (titles and/or editions): between 100 and 500.

Strengths:

Achievement   Education
Developmental   Reading

Historical Components/elements?: None Reported.

Minnesota School of Professional Psychology
Library
5503 Green Valley Drive
Bloomington, Minnesota 55437

Contact Person(s): Michael Khatib
E-mail address: MKhatib@PCLink.com
Telephone: 612-921-9500 ext.413
Fax number: 612-921-9863

Collection Access/Use

Tests may be used by: institutional faculty, graduate students, outside professionals, alumni.

Tests are available for: check-out to faculty/students, check-out to outside researchers.

Loan period: 2 days.

Collection Data

Size (titles and/or editions): between 100 and 500.

Strengths:

Achievement
Aptitude
Behavior Assessment

Neuropsychological
Personality

Historical Components/elements?: None Reported.

Minnesota

Minnesota State University - Mankato
Counseling and Student Personnel Department
Box 52
Mankato, Minnesota 56001

Contact Person(s): Dr. Diane H. Coursol
E-mail address: diane.coursol@mankato.msus.edu
Telephone: 507-389-5656
Fax number: 507-389-5074

Collection Access/Use

Tests may be used by: institutional faculty, graduate students.

Tests are available for: in-house use only, check-out to faculty/students, check-out with written approval.

Loan period: 24 hours.

Collection Data

Size (titles and/or editions): between 100 and 500.

Strengths:

Aptitude
Developmental
Education
Intelligence and Scholastic Aptitude

Multi-Aptitude Batteries
Personality
Sensory Motor
Vocations

Historical Components/elements?: None Reported.

University of Southern Mississippi
Gunn Educational Materials Center
USM Box 10071
Hattiesburg, Mississippi 39406

Contact Person(s): Todd Hively
E-mail address: Todd.Hively@usm.edu
Telephone: 601-266-4066
Fax number: 601-266-6033
Library/Collection Internet address(es):
  http://www.lib.usm.edu/gunn/gunn/html

Collection Access/Use

Tests may be used by: institutional faculty, graduate students, undergraduate students, outside professionals, general public.

Tests are available for: check-out to faculty/students.

Loan period: 2 weeks.

Collection Data

Size (titles and/or editions): between 100 and 500.

Strengths:

Behavior Assessment
Developmental

Sensory Motor
Speech & Hearing

General Information: ETS Tests in Microfiche.

Historical Components/elements?: None Reported.

Missouri

Harris-Stowe State College
Education Department
3026 Laclede Ave.
St. Louis, Missouri 63103

Contact Person(s): Eileen O'Brien
E-mail address: obriene@mail1.hssc.edu
Telephone: 314-340-3309
Fax number: 314-340-3555
Library/Collection Internet address(es):
    http://www.hssc.edu/library

Collection Access/Use

Tests may be used by: institutional faculty, undergraduate students.

Tests are available for: in-house use only, check-out to faculty/students.

Loan period: 1 semester.

Collection Data

Size (titles and/or editions): between 100 and 500.

Strengths:

Achievement
Behavior Assessment (just check lists; not really tests)
Developmental

English
Intelligence and Scholastic Aptitude
Reading

Historical components/elements?: Yes, we have the 1916 version of the Stanford Binet.

Southwest Baptist University
Library
1600 University Avenue
Bolivar, Missouri 65613

Contact Person(s): Betty Van Blair
E-mail address: bvanblai@sbuniv.edu
Telephone: 417-328-1622
Fax number: 417-328-1652
Library/Collection Internet address(es):
    http://library.sbuniv.edu
    telnet library.sbuniv.edu

Collection Access/Use

Tests may be used by: only those in certain classes.

Tests are available for: check-out with written approval.

Loan period: 2 hour in library use only.

Collection Data

Size (titles and/or editions): <100.

Historical Components/elements?: None Reported.

Missouri

Southwest Missouri State University
Curriculum Lab., Meyer Library
901 South National Avenue
Springfield, Missouri 65804-0095

Contact Person(s): Cherri Jones, Education Library
E-mail address: cgj229@mail.smsu.edu
Telephone: 417-836-4546
Fax number: 417-836-4764
Library/Collection Internet address(es):
> http://library.smsu.edu/Meyer/Curriculum/curriculum.html
> http://library.smsu.edu (click on ATLAS Online Catalog)

Collection Access/Use

Tests may be used by: institutional faculty, graduate students (those on a class list or with faculty permission), undergraduate students (those on a class list).

Tests are available for: in-house use only, check-out to faculty/students, check-out with written approval (students on class list can checkout as well).

Loan period: 1 week.

Collection Data

Size (titles and/or editions): between 100 and 500.

Strengths:

Aptitude
Developmental
Education

Reading
Speech & Hearing

Historical Components/elements?: None Reported.

University of Missouri - St. Louis
Ward E. Barnes Library
8001 Natural Bridge Rd.
St. Louis, Missouri 63121

Contact Person(s): Cheryle Cann or Peter Monat
E-mail address: cann@umsl.edu or pmonat@umsl.edu
Telephone: 314-516-5909 or 314-516-5571
Fax number: 314-516-6448 or 314-516-6468
Library/Collection Internet address(es):
    http://www.umsl.edu/services/library

Collection Access/Use

Tests may be used by: institutional faculty, graduate students, undergraduate students.

Tests are available for: in-house use only, check-out to faculty/students, check-out with written approval, for display to relevant campus class.

Loan period: two hour loan - in library use only.

Collection Data

Size (titles and/or editions): between 501-1000.

Strengths:

Achievement
Aptitude
Developmental
Education
Intelligence and Scholastic Aptitude
Mathematics

Multi-Aptitude Batteries
Personality
Reading
Speech & Hearing
Vocations

General Information: ETS Tests in Microfiche Collection is also included, as well as Mental Measurements Yearbook, Test Critiques and relevant test critique tools.

Historical Components/elements?: None Reported.

Missouri

University of Missouri - Columbia
Ellis Library, Reference
Columbia, Missouri 65201

Contact Person(s): Wayne Barnes
E-mail address: mulwbarn@showme.missouri.edu
Telephone: 573-882-3310
Fax number: 573-882-6034
Library/Collection Internet address(es):
   http://www.missouri.edu/~elliswww

Collection Access/Use

Tests may be used by: institutional faculty, graduate students, undergraduate students, outside professionals, general public.

Tests are available for: check-out to faculty/students, check-out with written approval, check-out to outside researchers.

Loan period: 1-7 days.

Collection Data

Size (titles and/or editions): between 1000 and 2000.

General Information: ETS Tests in Microfiche, Sets A-X.

Historical Components/elements?: None Reported.

Buros Institute of Mental Measurements
Library
104 Bancroft Hall
University of Nebraska-Lincoln
Lincoln, Nebraska 68588-0348

Contact Person(s): Janice Nelsen; Barbara Plake
E-mail address: bimm@unl.edu
Telephone: 402-472-6203
Fax number: 402-472-6207
Library/Collection Internet address(es):
   http://www.unl.edu/Buros

Collection Access/Use

Tests may be used by: institutional faculty, graduate students, undergraduate students, outside professionals, general public.

Tests are available for: in-house use only.

Collection Data

Size (titles and/or editions): 2000 or more.

Strengths:

Achievement
Aptitude
Behavior Assessment
Developmental
Education
English
Fine Arts
Foreign Languages
Intelligence and Scholastic Aptitude
Mathematics

Miscellaneous
Multi-Aptitude Batteries
Neuropsychological
Personality
Reading
Sensory Motor
Social Studies
Speech & Hearing
Vocations

Historical components/elements?: Yes, we have a limited number of out-of-print, very old, tests.

Nebraska

University of Nebraska - Kearney
Calvin T. Ryan Library
905 W 25th
Kearney, Nebraska 68849-2240

Contact Person(s): Janet Stoeger Wilke
E-mail address: wilkej@unk.edu
Telephone: 308-865-8546
Fax number: 308-865-8722
Library/Collection Internet address(es):
    http://rosi.unk.edu

Collection Access/Use

Tests may be used by: institutional faculty, graduate students, undergraduate students, outside professionals, general public.

Tests are available for: in-house use only (restricted tests may be used only by APA faculty members and the students they specify), check-out to faculty/students, check-out with written approval, check-out to outside researchers.

Loan period: 2 weeks.

Collection Data

Size (titles and/or editions): between 501-1000.

Strengths:

Behavior Assessment   Personality
Education   Reading

Historical components/elements?: No items are withdrawn, so the collection has historical components.

Plymouth State College
Lamson Library
Plymouth, New Hampshire 03264

Contact Person(s): Gary McCool
E-mail address: gmccool@mail.plymouth.edu
Telephone: 603-535-2457
Fax number: 603-535-2445
Library/Collection Internet address(es):
    http://www.plymouth.edu/psc/library

Collection Access/Use

Tests may be used by: institutional faculty, graduate students, undergraduate students.

Tests are available for: in-house use only, check-out to faculty/students, check-out with written approval, check-out to outside researchers.

Loan period: 3 days.

Collection Data

Size (titles and/or editions): between 100 and 500.

Strengths:

Achievement
Aptitude
Behavior Assessment
Developmental
Education
English
Fine Arts
Foreign Languages

Intelligence and Scholastic Aptitude
Mathematics
Multi-Aptitude Batteries
Personality
Reading
Sensory Motor
Vocations

General Information: All of our 379 tests are fully cataloged on our online catalog. Also, they may be seen by doing LC call number search under "LZ" (a unique category only used for tests).

Historical components/elements?: Yes, we have some old out-of-print tests and technical materials regarding construction of tests.

New Hampshire

Rivier College
Regina Library
420 Main St.
Nashua, New Hampshire

Contact Person(s): Donna Page
E-mail address: dpage@rivier.edu
Telephone: 603-897-8536
Fax number: 603-897-8889
Library/Collection Internet address(es):
> http://www.rivier.edu/departments/regina/reggie.htm
> http://library.rivier.edu

Collection Access/Use

Tests may be used by: institutional faculty, graduate students, undergraduate students, outside professionals.

Tests are available for: in-house use only, check-out with written approval.

Loan period: 1 week.

Collection Data

Size (titles and/or editions): between 100 and 500.

Strengths:

Achievement
Aptitude
Behavior Assessment
Developmental
Education
English
Mathematics

Multi-Aptitude Batteries
Personality
Reading
Sensory Motor
Speech & Hearing
Vocations

General Information: Restricted to use by Rivier students in pre-approved classes.

Historical components/elements?: Yes, older editions of some tests kept for comparative study.

Educational Testing Service
Carl Campbell Brigham Library
Test Collection 30-B
Princeton, New Jersey 08541

Contact Person(s): Pauline Stanley
E-mail address: library@ets.org
Telephone: 609-734-5689
Fax number: 609-683-7186
Library/Collection Internet address(es):
    http://ericae.net/Testcol.htm

Collection Access/Use

Tests may be used by: institutional faculty.

Tests are available for: check-out to faculty/students.

Loan period: 14 days.

Collection Data

Size (titles and/or editions): 20,000+

Strengths:

Achievement
Aptitude
Behavior Assessment
Developmental
Education
English
Fine Arts
Foreign Languages
Intelligence and Scholastic Aptitude
Mathematics

Miscellaneous
Multi-Aptitude Batteries
Neuropsychological
Personality
Reading
Sensory Motor
Social Studies
Speech & Hearing
Vocations

General Information: Given permission by the publisher, we can provide photocopies of out-of-print tests. Complete set of ETS Tests in Microfiche.

Historical components/elements?: Yes, we have tests going back to the early 1900s.

New Jersey

Montclair St. University
Curriculum Resource Center
001 Chapin Hall
Upper Montclair, New Jersey 07043

Contact Person(s): Pamela Gruchacz or Billy Wingren
E-mail address: gruchaczp@alpha.montclair.edu or wingrenw1@alpha.montclair.edu
Telephone: 973-655-5220
Fax number: 973-655-7776
Library/Collection Internet address(es):
    http://www.montclair.edu/Pages/CRC/CRC.html
    http://www.montclair.edu/Pages/CRC/Tests.html

Collection Access/Use

Tests may be used by: institutional faculty, graduate students, undergraduate students, outside professionals, general public.

Tests are available for: in-house use only.

Collection Data

Size (titles and/or editions): between 100 and 500.

Strengths:

Achievement
Aptitude
Education
English

Foreign Languages
Neuropsychological
Reading

Historical Components/elements?: None Reported.

Mount Saint Mary College
Education Building
360 Powell Ave.
Newburgh, New York 12550

Contact Person(s): Sr. Marion Beagen
E-mail address: beagen@msmc.edu
Telephone: 212-561-0800
Library/Collection Internet address(es):
　　http://www.msmc.edu:80/library

Collection Access/Use

Tests may be used by: institutional faculty, graduate students, undergraduate students.

Tests are available for: in-house use only (students), check-out to faculty/students (faculty only).

Loan period: Faculty may have tests for one semester.

Collection Data

Size (titles and/or editions): between 100 and 500.

Strengths:

Achievement
Behavior Assessment
Developmental
Intelligence and Scholastic Aptitude
Mathematics

Miscellaneous
Multi-Aptitude Batteries
Reading
Sensory Motor
Speech & Hearing

Historical Components/elements?: None Reported.

New York

Queens College - The City University of New York
Library
6530 Kissena Blvd.
Flushing, New York 11367

Contact Person(s): Suzanne D. Li
E-mail address: szi$lib@qc1.qc.edu
Telephone: 718-997-3774
Fax number: 718-997-3753
Library/Collection Internet address(es):
http://www.qc.edu/library

Collection Access/Use

Tests may be used by: institutional faculty, graduate students, undergraduate students.

Tests are available for: in-house use only.

Collection Data

Size (titles and/or editions): between 1000 and 2000.

General Information: ETS Tests in Microfiche, Sets A-X.

Historical components/elements?: Yes, collection has never been weeded.

Rochester Institute of Technology
Wallace Library-Reserve Desk
90 Lomb Memorial Drive
Rochester, New York 14623

Contact Person(s): Nykia M. Perez (Coordinator of Reserve Desk Service)
E-mail address: nmpwml@rit.edu
Telephone: 716-475-2025
Fax number: 716-475-7007
Library/Collection Internet address(es):
   http://wally.rit.edu

Collection Access/Use

Tests may be used by: institutional faculty, graduate students.

Tests are available for: check-out to faculty/students, check-out with written approval, check-out to outside researchers.

Loan period: 1 week.

Collection Data

Size (titles and/or editions): between 100 and 500.

Strengths:

Achievement
Aptitude
Behavior Assessment
Education
Mathematics

Multi-Aptitude Batteries
Personality
Reading
Speech & Hearing

Historical Components/elements?: None Reported.

New York

St. John's University
Instructional Materials Center
Rm. 429 Library
8000 Utopia Parkway
Jamaica, New York 11439

Contact Person(s): Connie Thorsen
E-mail address: thorsenc@stjohns.edu
Telephone: 718-990-5399
Fax number: 718-990-2071
Library/Collection Internet address(es):
 http://www.stjohns.edu

Collection Access/Use

Tests may be used by: institutional faculty, graduate students.

Tests are available for: in-house use only, check-out with written approval.

Collection Data

Size (titles and/or editions): between 100 and 500.

Strengths:

Achievement	Multi-Aptitude Batteries
Aptitude	Personality
Behavior Assessment	Reading
Education	Vocations

General Information: Tests may only be used for evaluation purposes. No copies can be made of any of the tests or the instruction booklets. Tests are used only in the center and may not be removed from the room. Test collection is searchable by card catalogue in center.

Historical components/elements?: Yes, we have older editions of tests.

State University of New York at Oswego
Lucy Wing Library
Mahar Hall
Oswego, New York 13126

Contact Person(s): Dr. Andrew Steinbrecher, Ph.D.
E-mail address: parsnow@oswego.edu
Telephone: 315-341-4051
Fax number: 315-341-3198

Collection Access/Use

Tests may be used by: institutional faculty, graduate students.

Tests are available for: check-out to faculty/students, check-out with written approval (very occasionally), check-out to outside researchers (very occasionally).

Loan period: 1 semester typically.

Collection Data

Size (titles and/or editions): between 100 and 500.

Strengths:

Achievement
Aptitude
Behavior Assessment
Mathematics

Multi-Aptitude Batteries
Personality
Reading
Vocations

Historical Components/elements?: None Reported.

New York

Teachers College of Columbia University
Milbank Memorial Library
525 W. 120th St.
New York, New York 10027

Contact Person(s): Jennifer Govan; David Ment
E-mail address: jennifer@edunet.tc.columbia.edu; david@edunet.tc.columbia.edu
Telephone: 212-678-3022; 212-678-4101
Fax number: 212-678-3092
Library/Collection Internet address(es):
   http://web.tc.columbia.edu

Collection Access/Use

Tests may be used by: institutional faculty, graduate students, undergraduate students (Columbia University affiliates), outside professionals, general public (with referral or appointment).

Tests are available for: in-house use only.

Collection Data

Size (titles and/or editions): between 100 and 500 (Main Collection), 2000 or more (Special Collections).

Strengths:

Achievement
Aptitude
Behavior Assessment
Developmental
Education
English
Fine Arts
Foreign Languages
Intelligence and Scholastic Aptitude
Mathematics

Miscellaneous
Multi-Aptitude Batteries
Neuropsychological
Personality
Reading
Sensory Motor
Social Studies
Speech & Hearing
Vocations

General Information: The Library subscribes to the ETS Test Collection on microfiche (ETS Tests in Microfiche) and collects extensive reference materials on tests and measurements.

Historical components/elements?: Yes, Special Collections maintains an historical collection of about 3,000 tests of all types, including aptitude, achievement, and skills, published from the late 1910s through the 1980s. Also held by Special Collections are the Edward L. Thorndike Papers, consisting of his annotated testing materials.

North Carolina

Campbell University
Curriculum Materials/Media Center
P.O. Box 309
Buies Creek, North Carolina 27506

Contact Person(s): Sharron Bortz
E-mail address: bortz@camel.campbell.edu
Telephone: 910-893-1595
Fax number: 910-893-1470
Library/Collection Internet address(es):
　　http://camel.campbell.edu/~kwok/

Collection Access/Use

Tests may be used by: institutional faculty, graduate students, undergraduate students.

Tests are available for: in-house use only.

Collection Data

Size (titles and/or editions): between 100 and 500.

Strengths:

Achievement
Aptitude
Behavior Assessment
Developmental
Education
English
Fine Arts
Intelligence and Scholastic Aptitude

Miscellaneous
Neuropsychological
Personality
Reading
Sensory Motor
Vocations
Learning Disabilities, Interest Inventories,
Marital/Family Assessment, Attitude

Historical components/elements?: Yes, we have tests going back as far as 1948.

North Carolina State University
Learning Resources Library
400 Poe Hall
Box 7801
Raleigh, North Carolina 27695-7801

Contact Person(s): Margaret Ann Link
E-mail address: Margaret_Link@ncsu.edu
Telephone: 919-515-3191
Fax number: 919-515-7634
Library/Collection Internet address(es):
    http://www2.ncsu.edu/ncsu/cep/lrl

Collection Access/Use

Tests may be used by: institutional faculty, graduate students, undergraduate students, outside professionals (in-house use only).

Tests are available for: in-house use only, check-out to faculty/students.

Loan period: 30 days.

Collection Data

Size (titles and/or editions): between 501-1000.

Strengths:

Intelligence and Scholastic Aptitude   Vocations
Personality   Career

Historical components/elements?: Yes, test publication dates span 1919-present. Over 100 tests published before 1950 (includes personality, intelligence, achievement, aptitude, and more).

North Carolina

University of North Carolina - Charlotte
J. Murrey Atkins Library
9201 University City Blvd.
Charlotte, North Carolina 28223-0001

Contact Person(s): Judy Walker, Curriculum Materials Librarian
E-mail address: jwalker@email.uncc.edu
Telephone: 704-547-2559
Library/Collection Internet address(es):
   http://libweb.uncc.edu/library
   All the materials are in our online catalog: http://jasmine.uncc.edu. They all start with the
   same classification (LB3060.33) and then are listed alphabetically by title.

Collection Access/Use

Tests may be used by: institutional faculty, graduate students, undergraduate students.

Tests are available for: in-house use only, check-out to faculty/students, check-out with
written approval, check-out to outside researchers (Although we do not usually check-out to
outside researchers, we will make accommodations for in-house use, if proper identification
and valid reasons for the research are given).

Loan period: 3 days with no renewals.

Collection Data

Size (titles and/or editions): between 100 and 500.

Strengths:

Achievement	Intelligence and Scholastic Aptitude
Aptitude	Mathematics
Behavior Assessment	Reading
Developmental	Vocations
Education	English as a Second Language (ESL)

General Information: We do have the ETS Tests in Microfiche collection. A web page
http://libweb.uncc.edu/ref-educ/tests.htm explains how to find tests in our collection and
background information on our collections.

Historical Components/elements?: None Reported.

Western Carolina University
Hunter Library-CMC
Cullowhee, North Carolina 28779

Contact Person(s): Elizabeth Vihnanek
E-mail address: vihnanek@wcu.edu
Telephone: 828-227-3493
Library/Collection Internet address(es):
　　http://wcu.edu/library

Collection Access/Use

　　Tests may be used by: institutional faculty, graduate students, undergraduate students.

　　Tests are available for: check-out to faculty/students.

　　Loan period: 2 weeks.

Collection Data

Size (titles and/or editions): <100.

Strengths:

NC Competency Tests

Historical Components/elements?: None Reported.

Ohio

Kent State University
College of Education, Instructional Resources Center
221 White Hall
Kent, Ohio 44242

Contact Person(s): Mary Tipton
E-mail address: mtipton@kent.edu
Telephone: 330-672-2256
Fax number: 330-672-7839
Library/Collection Internet address(es):
> http://coecatalog.educ.kent.edu/winnebago

Collection Access/Use

Tests may be used by: institutional faculty, graduate students, undergraduate students.

Tests are available for: in-house use only, check-out to faculty/students, check-out with written approval.

Loan period: one week.

Collection Data

Size (titles and/or editions): Between 100 and 500.

Strengths:

Achievement
Aptitude
Behavior Assessment
Developmental
Education
Intelligence and Scholastic Aptitude
Mathematics

Miscellaneous
Multi-Aptitude Batteries
Personality
Reading
Sensory Motor
Vocations

General Information: Some tests have computer scoring software that requires in-house use.

Historical components/elements?: Yes, copies of some older tests have been retained.

Lake Erie College
Lincoln Library
391 W. Washington Street
Painesville, Ohio 44077

Contact Person(s): Christopher Bennett
E-mail address: bennett@lakeerie.edu
Telephone: 440-639-7865
Fax number: 440-639-7865
Library/Collection Internet address(es):
http://www.lec.edu/library/index.stm

Collection Access/Use

Tests may be used by: institutional faculty, graduate students.

Tests are available for: in-house use only, check-out to faculty/students (faculty only).

Loan period: end of semester (faculty only).

Collection Data

Size (titles and/or editions): between 100 and 500.

Strengths:

Achievement   Reading

Historical Components/elements?: None Reported.

Ohio

Miami University
King Library
Instructional Materials Center
Oxford, Ohio 45056

Contact Person(s): Ruth Miller
Telephone: 513-529-2116
Fax number: 513-529-1719
Library/Collection Internet address(es):
   http://www.lib.muohio.edu

Collection Access/Use

Tests may be used by: institutional faculty, graduate students, undergraduate students.

Tests are available for: check-out to faculty/students.

Loan period: 1 week, no renewals.

Collection Data

Size (titles and/or editions): between 100 and 500.

Strengths:

Education   Reading

General Information: ETS Tests in Microfiche. Collection is only available to Miami University
faculty and students.

Historical Components/elements?: None Reported.

Notre Dame College (Ohio)
Clara Fritzsche Library
4545 College Rd.
South Euclid, Ohio 44121

Contact Person(s): Pat Peyton
E-mail address: ppeyton@ndc.edu
Telephone: 216-381-1680 ext.358
Fax number: 216-381-3227
Library/Collection Internet address(es):
   http://www.ndc.edu

Collection Access/Use

Tests may be used by: institutional faculty, graduate students, undergraduate students, outside professionals, general public.

Tests are available for: check-out to faculty/students, check-out to outside researchers.

Loan period: 3 weeks.

Collection Data

Size (titles and/or editions): between 100 and 500.

Strengths:

Achievement
English
Intelligence and Scholastic Aptitude

Mathematics
Reading
Social Studies

Historical Components/elements?: None Reported.

Ohio

Ohio State University
Education, Human Ecology, Psychology & Social Work Library
110 Sullivant Hall
1813 North High St.
Columbus, Ohio 43210-1307

Contact Person(s): Laura Gavrelis Blomquist
E-mail address: laura+@osu.edu; ehslib@osu.edu
Telephone: 614-292-8602
Fax number: 614-292-8012
Library/Collection Internet address(es):
 http://www.lib.ohio-state.edu/ehslib

Collection Access/Use

Tests may be used by: institutional faculty, graduate students, undergraduate students (with written request from faculty), outside professionals (current imprints-no; Historical-yes).

Tests are available for: in-house use only, check-out to faculty/students (in-house only), check-out with written approval (Few hours or overnight for class use).

Loan period: Usually a few hours, occasionally overnight for 7:30 a.m. classes.

Collection Data

Size (titles and/or editions):
between 100 and 500 (Current editions), 2000 or more ("Historical" instruments)

Strengths:

Achievement
Aptitude
Behavior Assessment
Developmental
Education
English
Fine Arts
Intelligence and Scholastic Aptitude
Mathematics

Miscellaneous
Multi-Aptitude Batteries
Neuropsychological
Personality
Reading
Sensory Motor
Social Studies
Speech & Hearing
Vocations

General Information: We also have the ETS Tests in Microfiche set. Because these are not standardized, they are available to the general public as well as OSU faculty and students for in-house usage. At this time, they are considered reference sources and do not circulate.

Historical components/elements?: Yes, we have more than 2000 test instruments from earlier times (e.g., the precursors to the SAT, individual and group tests in the categories covered in MMY). When we update a "current" test, we usually transfer the superseded edition to the historical file.

Ohio

Shawnee State University
Clark Memorial Library Instructional Materials Center
940 Second St.
Portsmouth, Ohio 45662

Contact Person(s): Mary Cummings; Bill Hannah
E-mail address: mcummings@shawnee.edu; bhannah@shawnee.edu
Telephone: 740-355-2513
Fax number: 740-355-2432
Library/Collection Internet address(es):
    http://beartrack.shawnee.edu

Collection Access/Use

Tests may be used by: institutional faculty, graduate students, undergraduate students, outside professionals, general public.

Tests are available for: in-house use only (students and community borrowers), check-out to faculty/students (faculty only)

Loan period: academic quarter.

Collection Data

Size (titles and/or editions): <100.

Historical Components/elements?: None Reported.

University of Akron
Archives of the History of American Psychology
Polsky Building, LL10-A
Akron, Ohio 44325-4302

Contact Person(s): Dr. David B. Baker
E-mail address: Bakerd@uakron.edu
Telephone: 330-972-7285
Fax number: 330-972-2093

Collection Access/Use

Tests may be used by: institutional faculty, graduate students, undergraduate students, outside professionals.

Tests are available for: in-house use only.

Collection Data

Size (titles and/or editions): 2000 or more.

Strengths:

Achievement
Aptitude
Behavior Assessment
Developmental
Education
Multi-Aptitude Batteries

Neuropsychological
Personality
Reading
Sensory Motor
Vocations

General Information: We hope to catalog the test collection in the next year.

Historical components/elements?: Yes, this collection of tests (5,000+) are part of the holdings of the Archives of the History of American Psychology (AHAP). The test collection is used for archival purposes and is used on-site by researchers.

Ohio

University of Dayton
School of Education, Curriculum Materials Center
103 Chaminade Hall
300 College Park Avenue
Dayton, Ohio 48885

Contact Person(s): Mrs. Ann M. Raney
E-mail address: Ann.Raney@notes.udayton.edu
Telephone: 937-229-3140
Fax number: 937-229-3199
Library/Collection Internet address(es):
> http://www.udayton.edu/~library

Collection Access/Use

> **Tests may be used by:** institutional faculty, graduate students, undergraduate students, outside professionals, general public.

> **Tests are available for:** check-out to faculty/students, check-out to outside researchers.

> **Loan period:** 3 weeks (undergraduate students), 2 months (graduate students), 6 months (faculty/staff).

Collection Data

Size (titles and/or editions): between 100 and 500.

Strengths:

Achievement	Mathematics
Aptitude	Personality
Developmental	Reading
Education	Sensory Motor
English	Learning Styles

Historical Components/elements?: None Reported.

Western Oregon University
Library
345 N. Monmouth Ave.
Monmouth, Oregon 97361

Contact Person(s): Peggy S. Cooper
E-mail address: cooperp@wou.edu
Telephone: 503-838-8890
Fax number: 503-838-8399
Library/Collection Internet address(es):
> http://www.wou.edu/provost/library

Collection Access/Use

Tests may be used by: institutional faculty, graduate students, undergraduate students.

Tests are available for: in-house use only.

Collection Data

Size (titles and/or editions): between 100 and 500.

Strengths:

Education   Reading
Personality

Historical Components/elements?: None Reported.

Texas

Baylor University
Learning Resource Center
School of Education
208 Draper, P.O. Box 97302
Waco, Texas 76798

Contact Person(s): Dorothy Schleicher
E-mail address: Dorothy_Schleicher@baylor.edu
Telephone: 254-710-3114
Fax number: 254-710-3160
Library/Collection Internet address(es):
    http://www.baylor.edu/~SOE/LRC/frontpage.edu

Collection Access/Use

Tests may be used by: institutional faculty, graduate students, undergraduate students, outside professionals.

Tests are available for: in-house use only, check-out to faculty/students.

Loan period: 1 week.

Collection Data

Size (titles and/or editions): between 501-1000.

Strengths:

Achievement
Aptitude
Behavior Assessment
Developmental
Intelligence and Scholastic Aptitude

Miscellaneous
Multi-Aptitude Batteries
Personality
Reading
Vocations

Historical Components/elements?: None Reported.

Texas Tech University
Box 40002
Lubbock, Texas 79409

Contact Person(s): Brian Quinn
E-mail address: LIBACQ@lib.ttu.edu
Telephone: 806-742-2236
Library/Collection Internet address(es):
    http://www.lib.ttu.edu

Collection Access/Use

Tests may be used by: institutional faculty, graduate students, undergraduate students, outside professionals, general public.

Tests are available for: in-house use only.

Collection Data

Size (titles and/or editions): between 501-1000.

Strengths:

Education

General Information: Our collection is largely ETS Tests in Microfiche (complete set). No paper copies of tests are owned.

Historical Components/elements?: None Reported.

Texas

University of Houston
M.D. Anderson Library
Houston, Texas 77204-2091

Contact Person(s): Mark Bay, Education/Social Sciences Reference Librarian
E-mail address: mbay@uh.edu
Telephone: 713-743-9767
Fax number: 713-743-9778
Library/Collection Internet address(es):
    http://info.lib.uh.edu

Collection Access/Use

Tests may be used by: institutional faculty, graduate students, undergraduate students, outside professionals, general public.

Tests are available for: in-house use only.

Collection Data

Size (titles and/or editions):between 501-1000.

Strengths:

Achievement
Aptitude
Behavior Assessment

Developmental
Education
Personality

General Information: Have ETS Tests in Microfiche.

Historical Components/elements?: None Reported.

University of Texas at Austin
Perry-Castaneda Library, Periodical Room
General Libraries
Austin, Texas 78713-7330

Contact Person(s): Bill Kopplin; Philip Schwartz
E-mail address: wjkopplin@mail.utexas.edu
Telephone: 512-495-4268
Fax number: 512-495-4296
Library/Collection Internet address(es):
   http://www.lib.utexas.edu

Collection Access/Use

Tests may be used by: institutional faculty, graduate students, undergraduate students, outside professionals.

Tests are available for: in-house use only, check-out to faculty/students, check-out to outside researchers.

Loan period: two hours.

Collection Data

Size (titles and/or editions): between 100 and 500.

Strengths:

Achievement
Aptitude
Behavior Assessment
Developmental

Personality
Reading
Sensory Motor
Speech & Hearing

General Information: We do have the ETS Tests in Microfiche from which photocopies may be made. We are also a depository for ERIC documents and have both ERIC and PsycINFO databases available for the general public.

Historical Components/elements?: None Reported.

Utah

Utah State University
Psychology Community Clinic
2810 Old Main Hill
Logan , Utah 84322-2810

Contact Person(s): Amy Wilberg
Telephone: 435-797-3401

Collection Access/Use

Tests may be used by: institutional faculty, graduate students.

Tests are available for: check-out to faculty/students.

Loan period: 3 days.

Collection Data

Size (titles and/or editions): between 100 and 500.

Strengths:

Achievement
Aptitude
Behavior Assessment

Neuropsychological
Personality
Vocations

Historical Components/elements?: None Reported.

Regent University
Regent University Library
1000 Regent University Dr.
Virginia Beach, Virginia 23320

Contact Person(s): Sandra Yaegle
E-mail address: sandyae@regent.edu
Telephone: 757-226-4165
Library/Collection Internet address(es):
>   http://www.regent.edu/lib

Collection Access/Use

>   **Tests may be used by:** institutional faculty, graduate students.

>   **Tests are available for:** check-out to faculty/students.

Collection Data

Size (titles and/or editions): between 100 and 500.

Strengths:

Education
Multi-Aptitude Batteries
Neuropsychological

Personality
Reading

General Information: Limited collection. The schools of Education and Counseling also have tests that are under licensure.

Historical Components/elements?: None Reported.

Washington

University of Washington
Suzzallo Library, Curriculum Materials and Children's Literature Section
Box 352900
Seattle, Washington 98195

Contact Person(s): Kristine Tardiff
E-mail address: ktardiff@u.washington.edu
Telephone: 206-543-2725
Fax number: 206-685-8049
Library/Collection Internet address(es):
    http://www.lib.washington.edu/Curriculum

Collection Access/Use

Tests may be used by: institutional faculty, graduate students, outside professionals.

Tests are available for: in-house use only.

Collection Data

Size (titles and/or editions): 2000 or more.

Strengths:

Achievement	Education
Aptitude	Multi-Aptitude Batteries
Behavior Assessment	Personality

General Information: Use of the test area is restricted to in-library use only by graduate students, faculty, and professionals with relevant credentials. The test collection is not actively updated. A Test Reference area, including materials such as Mental Measurements Yearbook, is also available. We also receive ETS Tests in Microfiche.

Historical components/elements?: Collection has many older tests.

University of Wisconsin - Madison
CIMC
225 North Mills Street
Madison, Wisconsin 53706

Contact Person(s): Jo Ann Carr
E-mail address: carr@education.wisc.edu
Telephone: 608-263-4755
Fax number: 608-262-6050
Library/Collection Internet address(es):
   http://cimc.education.wisc.edu
   http://madcat.library.wisc.edu

Collection Access/Use

Tests may be used by: institutional faculty, graduate students, undergraduate students, outside professionals, general public.

Tests are available for: in-house use only, check-out to faculty/students, check-out with written approval, check-out to outside researchers.

Loan period: varies from 3 days to 4 weeks.

Collection Data

Size (titles and/or editions): between 1000 and 2000.

Strengths:

Achievement
Developmental
Intelligence and Scholastic Aptitude

Multi-Aptitude Batteries
Reading

General Information: The CIMC has the ETS Tests in Microfiche, Sets A-X as well as print titles. The print titles access is determined by recommended APA guidelines with some titles in the open stacks and available for four-week loan and many titles in closed stacks with access restricted to individuals with written authorization.

Historical components/elements?: None Reported.

Wisconsin

University of Wisconsin - Stout
Department of Education, School Counseling, & School Psychology
408 Education & Human Services
Menomonie, Wisconsin 54751

Contact Person(s): Jacalyn Weissenburger
E-mail address: weissenburg@uwstout.edu
Telephone: 745-232-1326

Collection Access/Use

Tests may be used by: institutional faculty, graduate students.

Tests are available for: in-house use only, check-out to faculty/students, check-out to outside researchers (some graduate students from other departments).

Loan period: 2 weeks.

Collection Data

Size (titles and/or editions): between 501-1000.

Strengths:

Achievement
Aptitude
Behavior Assessment
Developmental
Education
English
Mathematics
Miscellaneous

Multi-Aptitude Batteries
Neuropsychological
Personality
Reading
Sensory Motor
Social Studies
Speech & Hearing

Historical components/elements?: We have a test museum of intelligence, sensory-motor, and neuropsychology assessments.

Appendix A
Cover Letter and Survey

Cover Letter:

Dear Colleague:

The Ad hoc Committee on the Test Collection Directory of the Education and Behavioral Sciences Section (EBSS) of the Association of College and Research Libraries (ACRL) has been charged with compiling information for a directory of test collections to be published in 2000.

The proposed directory will be useful to librarians, researchers, and the general public by providing information about test collection locations, strengths of test collections, and availability of tests for on-site viewing, or, when permissible, borrowing of test materials.

We would like to include information about your test collection in the directory. If you do not currently have a test collection, please respond accordingly. If a test collection is maintained elsewhere at your institution, please direct this survey to the appropriate individual.

We encourage you to supply additional information about your collection as appropriate. If your collection has fewer than 100 tests, we would like to list the collection in a separate appendix with brief information about it rather than providing a full scale description. Please let us know if that is acceptable.

In order to publish the directory during spring or summer 2000, we would appreciate your response by May 7, 1999. We apologize for any duplicate postings or mailings of this request you may receive, and encourage you to respond to only one of the survey requests. If you have any questions, please direct them to the e-mail, FAX, telephone, or postal address listed below.

Sincerely,

Member,
EBSS Ad hoc Committee on the Test Collection Directory

SURVEY:

1. Name of Institution_____

Location of Collection (library, department, etc.) _____

Address _____

_____

_____

Contact Person(s)_____

Telephone_____ Fax number_____

E-mail address_____

Library/Collection Internet address_____

2. Type of Institution:
a. public college/university _____
b. private college/university _____
c. non-academic research institution _____
d. other, specify _____

3. How many test titles/editions do you add to your collection on average per year?
a. 0-10 ____
b. 11-50 ____
c. 51-100 ____
d. 101 or more ____

4. Budget: How much funding is usually spent for the test titles/editions per year?
a. less than $500 ____
b. between $500 and $1000 ____
c. between $1000 and $5000 ____
d. $5000 or more ____

5. Source of Budget:
a. general funds ____
b. specific budget line ____
c. other, specify _____

6. Professional/Support Staff/Student time allotted to test collection activities per month:
a. less than 5 hrs.____
b. between 5 and 10 hrs.____
c. 10 hrs. or more ____

7. Is the collection accessible to any of the following (check all that apply):
a. your faculty ___
b. your graduate students___
c. your undergraduate students ___
 d. outside professionals ___
 e. general public ____
 f. other ____

8. In your experience, how would you rank the frequency of use (mark 1 to indicate the most frequent users, and then 2, 3, and 4 to indicate less frequent users):
a. your faculty ___
b. your graduate students___
c. your undergraduate students ___
d. outside researchers ___

9. Is any portion of the collection available for (check all that apply):
a. in-house use only ____
b. check-out to faculty/students ___
c. check-out w/ written approval ___
d. check-out to outside researchers ___
e. other, explain _____

10. In your experience, how would you rank the kind of use (mark 1 to indicate the most frequent use, and then 2, 3, 4 and 5 indicate to less frequent use):
a. In-house review of tests _____
b. Administer test _____
c. Check-out to faculty/graduate students for research/study _____
d. Course related study of test (undergraduates) _____
e. Check out to outside researchers _____
f. other (explain) _____

11. If any of the materials can be checked out, what is the loan period?

_____

12. Can the index/catalog to the collection be searched remotely: yes ___ no ___

13. If YES to item 12, provide a web or telnet address
(if address is not listed above in item 1.)

_____

14. Collection size (titles and/or editions):
a. between 100 and 500 ___
b. between 500 and 1000 ___
c. between 1000 and 2000 ___
d. 2000 or more ___

15. Please check all of the categories below that represent the strength(s) of your collection (categories according to Mental Measurements Yearbook, 12th Ed.):

Achievement____   Multi-Aptitude Batteries ____
Behavior Assessment ____   Neuropsychological ____
Developmental ____   Personality ____
Education ____   Reading ____
English ____   Sensory Motor____
Fine Arts ____   Social Studies ____
Foreign Languages ____   Speech & Hearing ____
Intelligence and Scholastic Aptitude_____   Vocations ____
Mathematics____   Other, specify _____
Miscellaneous____

16. Does your collection have historical components/elements?
NO___
YES____
If yes, explain:

17. General Information. Please append any relevant/ancillary information that would assist in the description of your collection (e.g. ETS Tests in Microfiche Sets A-X, special circumstances or restrictions to collection, etc.):

18. Eventually, our committee would like to provide the test directory online as part of the Education and Behavioral Sciences Section (EBSS) of the Association of College & Research Libraries' web site. Would you permit your submitted information to be a part of this online directory?
YES ___
NO ___

Appendix B

Charts and Graphs

The following charts and graphs provide information on management and usage of test collections.

Type of Institution

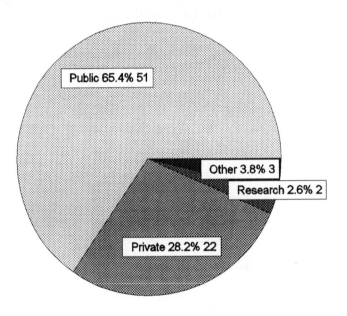

Public 65.4% 51

Other 3.8% 3

Research 2.6% 2

Private 28.2% 22

Average Number of Tests Added Annually

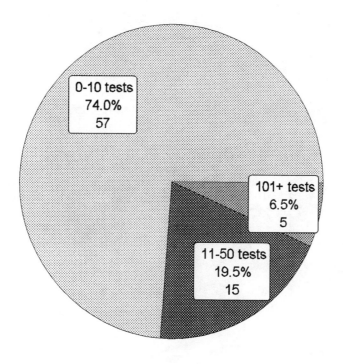

0-10 tests
74.0%
57

101+ tests
6.5%
5

11-50 tests
19.5%
15

Annual Budget for Test Purchases*

*percentages do not total 100% because of rounding

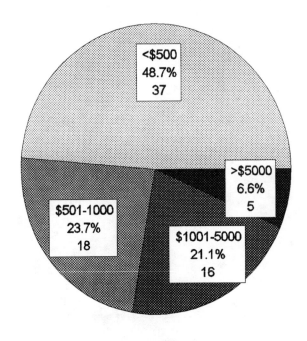

Professional/Support/Student Staffing

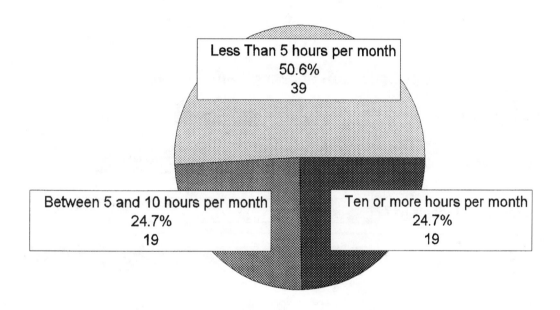

Less Than 5 hours per month
50.6%
39

Between 5 and 10 hours per month
24.7%
19

Ten or more hours per month
24.7%
19

☐ Less Than 5 hours per month
▦ Between 5 and 10 hours per month
■ Ten or more hours per month

Use of the Collection By Type of User and Ranked Level of Use

Rank	Faculty n=77	Graduate Students n=72	Undergraduates n=60	Outside Researchers n=43
1(high)	9	54	13	1
2	31	13	25	3
3	33	3	15	8
4(low)	4	2	7	31

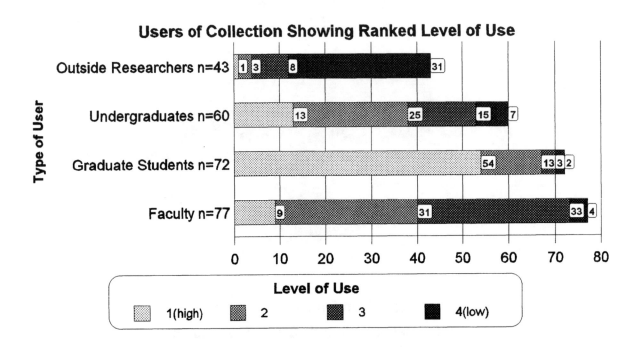

Users of Collection Showing Ranked Level of Use

Use of the Collection By Access Restrictions and Ranked Level of Use

Ranked Level of Use	In-house Review n=70	Administer n=41	Check out to Faculty/ Graduate Students n=55	Course-Related Study: Undergraduates n=57	Check Out to Outside Researchers n=23	Other n=5
1 (high)	35	7	23	17	0	
2	12	9	21	21	1	
3	15	11	7	14	1	
4	8	8	2	1	9	
5 (low)	0	6	2	4	12	

Use of the Collection

(By Access Restrictions and Ranked Level of Use)

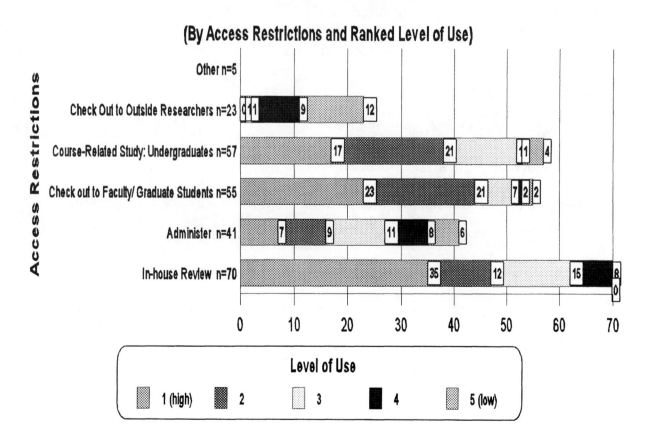

Indexes

The main directory is organized alphabetically by state, and for each state institutions are listed alphabetically. The following indexes offer additional access points to help identify appropriate collections. The page number in the main directory area follows the institution name in parentheses.

Alphabetical List of Institutions
Directory page numbers appear in parentheses

American College Testing (22)
Azusa Pacific University (1)
Baylor University (72)
Boston College (27)
Bridgewater State College (28)
Buros Institute of Mental Measurements (45)
California Polytechnic State University - San Luis Obispo (2)
California School of Professional Psychology - Fresno (3)
California School of Professional Psychology, Los Angeles Campus (4)
California State University - Chico (5)
California State University - Fullerton (6)
California State University - Long Beach (7)
Campbell University (58)
Chicago School of Professional Psychology (13)
Chicago State University (14)
Concordia University (Illinois) (15)
Concordia University (Minnesota) (36)
Educational Testing Service (49)
Florida International University (11)
Georgia School of Professional Psychology (12)
Harris-Stowe State College (40)
Harvard Graduate School of Education (29)
Illinois State University (16)
Indiana State University (21)
Kent State University (62)
Lake Erie College (63)
Miami University (64)
Minnesota School of Professional Psychology (37)
Minnesota State University - Mankato (38)
Montclair St. University (50)
Mount Saint Mary College (51)
North Carolina State University (59)
Notre Dame College (Ohio) (65)
Ohio State University (66)
Plymouth State College (47)
Queens College - The City University of New York (52)
Regent University (77)
Rivier College (48)
Rochester Institute of Technology (53)
Salem State College (30)

Shawnee State University (68)
Southern Illinois University at Carbondale (17)
Southwest Baptist University (41)
Southwest Missouri State University (42)
Spalding University (26)
State University of New York at Oswego (55)
St. John's University (54)
Teachers College of Columbia University (56)
Texas Tech University (73)
University of Akron (69)
University of Dayton (70)
University of Delaware (10)
University of Houston (74)
University of Illinois at Chicago (18)
University of Illinois at Urbana-Champaign (19)
University of Iowa (23)
University of Massachusetts - Boston (31)
University of Michigan (34)
University of Missouri - Columbia (44)
University of Missouri - St. Louis (43)
University of Nebraska - Kearney (46)
University of North Carolina - Charlotte (60)
University of Northern Colorado (8)
University of Northern Iowa (24)
University of Southern Colorado (9)
University of Southern Mississippi (39)
University of Texas at Austin (75)
University of Washington (78)
University of Wisconsin - Madison (79)
University of Wisconsin - Stout (80)
Utah State University (76)
Washburn University of Topeka (25)
Wayne State University (35)
Western Carolina University (61)
Western Oregon University (71)
Westfield State College (32)
Worcester State College (33)

Institutions with Searchable Catalogs/Indexes for Their Test Collections

Bridgewater State College
    http://www.bridgew.edu/depts/maxwell/currlib.htm

California State University - Chico
    http://www.csuchico.edu/library/index.html

California State University - Fullerton
    http://www.library.fullerton.edu

Concordia University (Minnesota)
    http://www.csp.edu/VirtualLibrary/

Educational Testing Service
    http://ericae.net/Testcol.htm

Florida International University
    http://www.fiu.edu/~library/assistance/uptests.html

Harvard Graduate School of Education
    http://hplus.harvard.edu

Indiana State University
    http://odin.indstate.edu

Kent State University
    http://coecatalog.educ.kent.edu/winnebago

Lake Erie College
    http://www.lec.edu/library/index.stm

Montclair St. University
    http://www.montclair.edu/Pages/CRC/Tests.html

Plymouth State College
    http://www.plymouth.edu/psc/library

Regent University
    http://www.regent.edu/lib

Rivier College
   http://library.rivier.edu

Shawnee State University
   http://beartrack.shawnee.edu

Southwest Baptist University
   telnet library.sbuniv.edu
   http://library.sbuniv.edu

Southwest Missouri State University
   http://library.smsu.edu (click on ATLAS Online Catalog)

University of Delaware
   http://www.udel.edu/erc

University of Illinois at Urbana/Champaign
   http://www.library.uiuc.edu/edx/testcoll/input.asp

University of North Carolina at Charlotte
   All the materials are in our online catalog: http://jasmine.uncc.edu. They all start with
   the same classification (LB3060.33) and then are listed alphabetically by title.

University of Southern Colorado
   http://www.uscolo.edu/library

University of Texas at Austin
   http://www.lib.utexas.edu

University of Wisconsin at Madison
   http://madcat.library.wisc.edu

Washburn University of Topeka
   http://lib.wuacc.edu

Western Carolina University
   http://wcu.edu/library

Institutions that Own Some or All of the ETS Tests in Microfiche Collection
Directory page numbers appear in parentheses

Azusa Pacific University (1)
Boston College (27)
Bridgewater State College (28)
California Polytechnic State University - San Luis Obispo (2)
California School of Professional Psychology, Los Angeles Campus (4)
California State University - Long Beach (7)
Educational Testing Service (49)
Harvard Graduate School of Education (29)
Illinois State University (16)
Indiana State University (21)
Miami University (64)
Ohio State University (66)
Queens College - The City University of New York (52)
Southern Illinois University at Carbondale (17)
Teachers College of Columbia University (56)
Texas Tech University (73)
University of Delaware (10)
University of Houston (74)
University of Illinois at Chicago (18)
University of Illinois at Urbana-Champaign (19)
University of Iowa (23)
University of Missouri - Columbia (44)
University of Missouri - St. Louis (43)
University of North Carolina - Charlotte (60)
University of Southern Mississippi (39)
University of Texas at Austin (75)
University of Washington (78)
University of Wisconsin - Madison (79)
Wayne State University (35)

Institutions Reporting Historical* Tests in Their Collections
Directory page numbers appear in parentheses

Buros Institute of Mental Measurements (45)
California School of Professional Psychology - Fresno (3)
California State University - Chico (5)
California State University - Fullerton (6)
California State University - Long Beach (7)
Campbell University (58)
Chicago School of Professional Psychology (13)
Chicago State University (14)
Educational Testing Service (49)
Harris-Stowe State College (40)
Harvard Graduate School of Education (29)
Kent State University (62)
North Carolina State University (59)
Ohio State University (66)
Plymouth State College (47)
Queens College - The City University of New York (52)
Rivier College (48)
Southern Illinois University at Carbondale (17)
St. John's University (54)
Teachers College of Columbia University (56)
University of Akron (69)
University of Delaware (10)
University of Illinois at Urbana-Champaign (19)
University of Iowa (23)
University of Michigan (34)
University of Nebraska - Kearney (46)
University of Northern Iowa (24)
University of Southern Colorado (9)
Wayne State University (35)
University of Washington (78)
University of Wisconsin - Stout (80)

*Historical tests include superseded versions/editions and other tests no longer available from a publisher. These tests are useful for historical and comparative research.

Size of Collections
Directory page numbers appear in parentheses

Fewer than 100 tests

Florida International University (11)
Shawnee State University (68)
Southwest Baptist University (41)
Western Carolina University (61)

Between 100 and 500 tests

Boston College (27)
California School of Professional Psychology - Fresno (3)
California School of Professional Psychology, Los Angeles Campus (4)
California State University - Chico (5)
California State University - Fullerton (6)
Campbell University (58)
Chicago School of Professional Psychology (13)
Chicago State University (14)
Concordia University (Illinois) (15)
Concordia University (Minnesota) (36)
Georgia School of Professional Psychology (12)
Harris-Stowe State College (40)
Kent State University (62)
Lake Erie College (63)
Miami University (64)
Minnesota School of Professional Psychology (37)
Minnesota State University - Mankato (38)
Montclair St. University (50)
Mount Saint Mary College (51)
Notre Dame College (Ohio) (65)
Ohio State University (Current collection) (66)
Plymouth State College (47)
Regent University (77)
Rivier College (48)
Rochester Institute of Technology (53)
Salem State College (30)
Southwest Missouri State University (42)
Spalding University (26)
St. John's University (54)
State University of New York at Oswego (55)
Teachers College of Columbia University (Main Collection) (56)
University of Dayton (70)
University of Massachusetts - Boston (31)

Between 100 and 500 tests (cont.)
    University of North Carolina - Charlotte (60)
    University of Southern Colorado (9)
    University of Southern Mississippi (39)
    University of Delaware (10)
    University of Northern Iowa (24)
    University of Texas at Austin (75)
    Utah State University (76)
    Washburn University of Topeka (25)
    Wayne State University (35)
    Western Oregon University (71)
    Westfield State College (32)
    Worcester State College (33)

Between 501 and 1000 tests
    American College Testing (22)
    Azusa Pacific University (1)
    Baylor University (72)
    Bridgewater State College (28)
    California Polytechnic State University - San Luis Obispo (2)
    Illinois State University (16)
    Indiana State University (21)
    North Carolina State University (59)
    Texas Tech University (73)
    University of Houston (74)
    University of Missouri - St. Louis (43)
    University of Nebraska - Kearney (46)
    University of Wisconsin - Stout (80)

Between 1000 and 2000 tests
    Queens College - The City University of New York (52)
    Southern Illinois University at Carbondale (17)
    University of Illinois at Chicago (18)
    University of Michigan (34)
    University of Missouri - Columbia (44)
    University of Northern Colorado (8)
    University of Wisconsin - Madison (79)

2000 or more tests
    Buros Institute of Mental Measurements (45)
    Educational Testing Service (49)
    Harvard Graduate School of Education (29)
    Ohio State University (Historical collection) (66)

2000 or more tests (cont.)
    Teachers College of Columbia University (Special Collections) (56)
    University of Akron (69)
    University of Illinois at Urbana-Champaign (19)
    University of Iowa (23)
    University of Washington (78)

Access to Tests - User Categories
Directory page numbers appear in parentheses

Alumni
>	Minnesota School of Professional Psychology (37)

Consortium members
>	University of Massachusetts - Boston (31)

General public
>	Boston College (27)
>	Bridgewater State College (28)
>	Buros Institute of Mental Measurements (45)
>	California State University - Long Beach (7)
>	Chicago State University (14)
>	Concordia University (Minnesota) (36)
>	Florida International University (11)
>	Harvard Graduate School of Education (29)
>	Illinois State University (16)
>	Mount Saint Mary College (51)
>	Ohio State University (Historical collection only) (66)
>	Plymouth State College (47)
>	Southern Illinois University at Carbondale (17)
>	University of Akron (69)
>	University of Delaware (10)
>	University of Houston (74)
>	University of Illinois at Chicago (18)
>	University of Illinois at Urbana-Champaign (19)
>	University of Iowa (23)
>	University of Nebraska - Kearney (46)
>	University of Northern Colorado (8)
>	University of Northern Iowa (24)
>	University of Southern Colorado (9)
>	University of Southern Mississippi (39)
>	University of Texas at Austin (75)
>	University of Wisconsin - Stout (80)
>	Utah State University (76)
>	Washburn University of Topeka (25)
>	Wayne State University (35)
>	Western Oregon University (71)
>	Worcester State College (33)

Graduate students

Azusa Pacific University (1)
Baylor University (72)
Boston College (27)
Bridgewater State College (28)
Buros Institute of Mental Measurements (45)
California Polytechnic State University - San Luis Obispo (2)
California School of Professional Psychology - Fresno (3)
California School of Professional Psychology, Los Angeles Campus (4)
California State University - Chico (5)
California State University - Fullerton (6)
California State University - Long Beach (7)
Chicago School of Professional Psychology (13)
Chicago State University (14)
Concordia University (Illinois) (15)
Concordia University (Minnesota) (36)
Educational Testing Service (49)
Florida International University (11)
Georgia School of Professional Psychology (12)
Harvard Graduate School of Education (29)
Illinois State University (16)
Indiana State University (21)
Kent State University (62)
Lake Erie College (63)
Miami University (64)
Minnesota School of Professional Psychology (37)
Minnesota State University - Mankato (38)
Mount Saint Mary College (51)
North Carolina State University (59)
Notre Dame College (Ohio) (65)
Ohio State University (66)
Plymouth State College (47)
Queens College - The City University of New York (52)
Regent University (77)
Rivier College (48)
Rochester Institute of Technology (53)
Salem State College (30)
Southern Illinois University at Carbondale (17)
Spalding University (26)
St. John's University (54)
State University of New York at Oswego (55)
Teachers College of Columbia University (56)
Texas Tech University (73)

Graduate students (cont.)

University of Akron (69)
University of Dayton (70)
University of Delaware (10)
University of Houston (74)
University of Illinois at Chicago (18)
University of Illinois at Urbana-Champaign (19)
University of Iowa (23)
University of Massachusetts - Boston (31)
University of Michigan (34)
University of Missouri - Columbia (44)
University of Missouri - St. Louis (43)
University of Nebraska - Kearney (46)
University of North Carolina - Charlotte (60)
University of Northern Colorado (8)
University of Northern Iowa (24)
University of Southern Colorado (9)
University of Southern Mississippi (39)
University of Texas at Austin (75)
University of Washington (78)
University of Wisconsin - Madison (79)
University of Wisconsin - Stout (80)
Utah State University (76)
Washburn University of Topeka (25)
Wayne State University (35)
Western Carolina University (61)
Western Oregon University (71)
Westfield State College (32)
Worcester State College (33)

Institutional faculty

American College Testing (22)
Azusa Pacific University (1)
Baylor University (72)
Boston College (27)
Bridgewater State College (28)
Buros Institute of Mental Measurements (45)
California Polytechnic State University - San Luis Obispo (2)
California School of Professional Psychology - Fresno (3)
California School of Professional Psychology, Los Angeles Campus (4)
California State University - Chico (5)
California State University - Fullerton (6)
California State University - Long Beach (7)

Institutional faculty (cont.)

    Chicago School of Professional Psychology (13)
    Chicago State University (14)
    Concordia University (Illinois) (15)
    Concordia University (Minnesota) (36)
    Educational Testing Service (49)
    Florida International University (11)
    Georgia School of Professional Psychology (12)
    Harris-Stowe State College (40)
    Harvard Graduate School of Education (29)
    Illinois State University (16)
    Indiana State University (21)
    Kent State University (62)
    Lake Erie College (63)
    Miami University (64)
    Minnesota School of Professional Psychology (37)
    Minnesota State University - Mankato (38)
    Montclair St. University (50)
    Mount Saint Mary College (51)
    North Carolina State University (59)
    Notre Dame College (Ohio) (65)
    Ohio State University (66)
    Plymouth State College (47)
    Queens College - The City University of New York (52)
    Regent University (77)
    Rivier College (48)
    Rochester Institute of Technology (53)
    Salem State College (30)
    Southern Illinois University at Carbondale (17)
    Spalding University (26)
    St. John's University (54)
    State University of New York at Oswego (55)
    Teachers College of Columbia University (56)
    Texas Tech University (73)
    University of Akron (69)
    University of Dayton (70)
    University of Delaware (10)
    University of Houston (74)
    University of Illinois at Chicago (18)
    University of Illinois at Urbana-Champaign (19)
    University of Iowa (23)
    University of Massachusetts - Boston (31)
    University of Michigan (34)

Institutional faculty (cont.)
University of Missouri - Columbia (44)
University of Missouri - St. Louis (43)
University of Nebraska - Kearney (46)
University of North Carolina - Charlotte (60)
University of Northern Colorado (8)
University of Northern Iowa (24)
University of Southern Colorado (9)
University of Southern Mississippi (39)
University of Texas at Austin (75)
University of Washington (78)
University of Wisconsin - Madison (79)
University of Wisconsin - Stout (80)
Utah State University (76)
Washburn University of Topeka (25)
Wayne State University (35)
Western Carolina University (61)
Western Oregon University (71)
Westfield State College (32)
Worcester State College (33)

Only those in certain classes
Southwest Baptist University (41)

Outside professionals
Boston College (27)
Bridgewater State College (28)
Buros Institute of Mental Measurements (45)
California Polytechnic State University - San Luis Obispo (2)
California State University - Fullerton (6)
California State University - Long Beach (7)
Chicago School of Professional Psychology (13)
Chicago State University (14)
Concordia University (Minnesota) (36)
Educational Testing Service (49
Florida International University (11)
Harvard Graduate School of Education (29)
Illinois State University (16)
Indiana State University (21)
Minnesota School of Professional Psychology (37)
Mount Saint Mary College (51)
Ohio State University (66)
Plymouth State College (47)

Outside professionals (cont.)

Southern Illinois University at Carbondale (17)
Texas Tech University (73)
University of Akron (69)
University of Dayton (70)
University of Delaware (10)
University of Houston (74)
University of Illinois at Chicago (18)
University of Illinois at Urbana-Champaign (19)
University of Iowa (23)
University of Massachusetts - Boston (31)
University of Nebraska - Kearney (46)
University of North Carolina - Charlotte (60)
University of Northern Colorado (8)
University of Northern Iowa (24)
University of Southern Colorado (9)
University of Southern Mississippi (39)
University of Texas at Austin (75)
University of Wisconsin - Madison (79)
University of Wisconsin - Stout (80)
Utah State University (76)
Washburn University of Topeka (25)
Western Oregon University (71)
Worcester State College (33)
Wayne State University (35)

Staff

American College Testing (22)
California State University - Chico (5)
Western Oregon University (71)

Undergraduate students

Azusa Pacific University (1)
Baylor University (72)
Boston College (27)
Bridgewater State College (28)
Buros Institute of Mental Measurements (45)
California Polytechnic State University - San Luis Obispo (2)
California State University - Chico (5)
California State University - Fullerton (6)
California State University - Long Beach (7)
Chicago State University (14)
Concordia University (Illinois) (15)

Undergraduate students (cont.)
    Concordia University (Minnesota) (36)
    Educational Testing Service (49)
    Florida International University (11)
    Harris-Stowe State College (40)
    Harvard Graduate School of Education (29)
    Illinois State University (16)
    Indiana State University (21)
    Kent State University (62)
    Lake Erie College (63)
    Mount Saint Mary College (51)
    North Carolina State University (59)
    Notre Dame College (Ohio) (65)
    Ohio State University (66)
    Plymouth State College (47)
    Queens College - The City University of New York (52)
    Rivier College (48)
    Rochester Institute of Technology (53)
    Salem State College (30)
    Southern Illinois University at Carbondale (17)
    Spalding University (26)
    Texas Tech University (73)
    University of Akron (69)
    University of Dayton (70)
    University of Delaware (10)
    University of Houston (74)
    University of Illinois at Chicago (18)
    University of Illinois at Urbana-Champaign (19)
    University of Iowa (23)
    University of Missouri - Columbia (44)
    University of Missouri - St. Louis (43)
    University of Nebraska - Kearney (46)
    University of North Carolina - Charlotte (60)
    University of Northern Colorado (8)
    University of Northern Iowa (24)
    University of Southern Colorado (9)
    University of Southern Mississippi (39)
    University of Texas at Austin (75)
    University of Wisconsin - Stout (80)
    Utah State University (76)
    Washburn University of Topeka (25)
    Wayne State University (35)
    Western Carolina University (61)

Undergraduate students (cont.)
Western Oregon University (71)
Westfield State College (32)
Worcester State College (33)

Access to Tests - Local Restrictions
Directory page numbers appear in parentheses

Check-out to faculty/students
American College Testing (22)
Azusa Pacific University (1)
Baylor University (72)
Boston College (27)
California Polytechnic State University - San Luis Obispo (2)
California School of Professional Psychology - Fresno (3)
California School of Professional Psychology, Los Angeles Campus (4)
California State University - Fullerton (6)
Chicago School of Professional Psychology (13)
Concordia University (Minnesota) (36)
Educational Testing Service (49)
Georgia School of Professional Psychology (12)
Harris-Stowe State College (40)
Kent State University (62)
Lake Erie College (63)
Miami University (64)
Minnesota School of Professional Psychology (37)
Minnesota State University - Mankato (38)
Mount Saint Mary College (51)
North Carolina State University (59)
Notre Dame College (Ohio) (65)
Ohio State University (66)
Plymouth State College (47)
Regent University (77)
Rochester Institute of Technology (53)
Shawnee State University (68)
Spalding University (26)
Southwest Missouri State University (42)
State University of New York at Oswego (55)
University of Dayton (70)
University of Delaware (10)
University of Iowa (23)
University of Massachusetts - Boston (31)
University of Michigan (34)
University of Missouri - Columbia (44)
University of Missouri - St. Louis (43)
University of Nebraska - Kearney (46)
University of North Carolina - Charlotte (60)
University of Northern Colorado (8)

Check-out to faculty/students (cont.)
University of Northern Iowa (24)
University of Southern Mississippi (39)
University of Texas at Austin (75)
University of Wisconsin - Madison (79)
University of Wisconsin - Stout (80)
Utah State University (76)
Washburn University of Topeka (25)
Western Carolina University (61)

Check-out to outside researchers
Minnesota School of Professional Psychology (37)
Notre Dame College (Ohio) (65)
Plymouth State College (47)
Rochester Institute of Technology (53)
State University of New York at Oswego (55)
University of North Carolina - Charlotte (60)
University of Dayton (70)
University of Iowa (23)
University of Missouri - Columbia (44)
University of Nebraska - Kearney (46)
University of Northern Colorado (8)
University of Northern Iowa (24)
University of Texas at Austin (75)
University of Wisconsin - Madison (79)
University of Wisconsin - Stout (80)
Washburn University of Topeka (25)

Check-out with written approval
Azusa Pacific University (1)
California Polytechnic State University - San Luis Obispo (2)
California State University - Chico (5)
California State University - Fullerton (6)
Concordia University (Illinois) (15)
Illinois State University (16)
Indiana State University (21)
Kent State University (62)
Minnesota State University - Mankato (38)
Ohio State University (66)
Plymouth State College (47)
Rivier College (48)
Rochester Institute of Technology (53)
Salem State College (30)

Check-out with written approval (cont.)

    Southwest Baptist University (41)
    Southwest Missouri State University (42)
    St. John's University (54)
    State University of New York at Oswego (55)
    University of Delaware (10)
    University of Massachusetts - Boston (31)
    University of Michigan (34)
    University of Missouri - Columbia (44)
    University of Missouri - St. Louis (43)
    University of Nebraska - Kearney (46)
    University of North Carolina - Charlotte (60)
    University of Northern Colorado (8)
    University of Wisconsin - Madison (79)
    Washburn University of Topeka (25)
    Westfield State College (32)

In-house use only

    Baylor University (72)
    Boston College (27)
    Bridgewater State College (28)
    Buros Institute of Mental Measurements (45)
    California School of Professional Psychology - Fresno (3)
    California School of Professional Psychology, Los Angeles Campus (4)
    California State University - Fullerton (6)
    California State University - Long Beach (7)
    Campbell University (58)
    Chicago School of Professional Psychology (13)
    Chicago State University (14)
    Florida International University (11)
    Georgia School of Professional Psychology (12)
    Harris-Stowe State College (40)
    Harvard Graduate School of Education (29)
    Indiana State University (21)
    Illinois State University (16)
    Kent State University (62)
    Lake Erie College (63)
    Minnesota State University - Mankato (38)
    Montclair St. University (50)
    Mount Saint Mary College (51)
    North Carolina State University (59)
    Ohio State University (66)
    Plymouth State College (47)

In-house use only (cont.)

    Queens College - The City University of New York (52)
    Rivier College (48)
    Shawnee State University (68)
    Southern Illinois University at Carbondale (17)
    Southwest Missouri State University (42)
    Spalding University (26)
    St. John's University (54)
    Teachers College of Columbia University (56)
    Texas Tech University (73)
    University of Akron (69)
    University of Delaware (10)
    University of Houston (74)
    University of Illinois at Chicago (18)
    University of Illinois at Urbana-Champaign (19)
    University of Massachusetts - Boston (31)
    University of Missouri - St. Louis (43)
    University of Nebraska - Kearney (46)
    University of North Carolina - Charlotte (60)
    University of Northern Colorado (8)
    University of Northern Iowa (24)
    University of Southern Colorado (9)
    University of Texas at Austin (75)
    University of Washington (78)
    University of Wisconsin - Madison (79)
    University of Wisconsin - Stout (80)
    Washburn University of Topeka (25)
    Wayne State University (35)
    Western Oregon University (71)
    Worcester State College (33)

Strengths of Test Collections (Mental Measurements Yearbook Categories)
Directory page numbers appear in parentheses

Achievement

American College Testing (22)
Azusa Pacific University (1)
Baylor University (72)
Bridgewater State College (28)
Buros Institute of Mental Measurements (45)
California Polytechnic State University - San Luis Obispo (2)
California School of Professional Psychology - Fresno (3)
California State University - Chico (5)
Campbell University (58)
Chicago School of Professional Psychology (13)
Chicago State University (14)
Concordia University (Illinois) (15)
Concordia University (Minnesota) (36)
Educational Testing Service (49)
Florida International University (11)
Georgia School of Professional Psychology (12)
Harris-Stowe State College (40)
Harvard Graduate School of Education (29)
Illinois State University (16)
Kent State University (62)
Lake Erie College (63)
Minnesota School of Professional Psychology (37)
Montclair St. University (50)
Mount Saint Mary College (51)
North Carolina State University (59)
Notre Dame College (Ohio) (65)
Ohio State University (66)
Plymouth State College (47)
Rivier College (48)
Rochester Institute of Technology (53)
Salem State College (30)
Southern Illinois University at Carbondale (17)
Spalding University (26)
St. John's University (54)
State University of New York at Oswego (55)
Teachers College of Columbia University (56)
University of Akron (69)
University of Dayton (70)
University of Delaware (10)

Achievement (cont.)
- University of Houston (74)
- University of Illinois at Chicago (18)
- University of Illinois at Urbana-Champaign (19)
- University of Iowa (23)
- University of Massachusetts - Boston (31)
- University of Missouri - St. Louis (43)
- University of North Carolina - Charlotte (60)
- University of Northern Colorado (8)
- University of Northern Iowa (24)
- University of Texas at Austin (75)
- University of Washington (78)
- University of Wisconsin - Madison (79)
- University of Wisconsin - Stout (80)
- Utah State University (76)
- Washburn University of Topeka (25)
- Wayne State University (35)
- Westfield State College (32)
- Worcester State College (33)

Aptitude
- American College Testing (22)
- Azusa Pacific University (1)
- Baylor University (72)
- Boston College (27)
- Bridgewater State College (28)
- Buros Institute of Mental Measurements (45)
- California Polytechnic State University - San Luis Obispo (2)
- California School of Professional Psychology - Fresno (3)
- California State University - Chico (5)
- California State University - Long Beach (7)
- Campbell University (58)
- Chicago School of Professional Psychology (13)
- Chicago State University (14)
- Concordia University (Illinois) (15)
- Educational Testing Service (49)
- Florida International University (11)
- Georgia School of Professional Psychology (12)
- Harris-Stowe State College (40)
- Harvard Graduate School of Education (29)
- Illinois State University (16)
- Kent State University (62)
- Minnesota School of Professional Psychology (37)

Aptitude (cont.)

    Minnesota State University - Mankato (38)
    Montclair St. University (50)
    Mount Saint Mary College (51)
    North Carolina State University (59)
    Notre Dame College (Ohio) (65)
    Ohio State University (66)
    Plymouth State College (47)
    Regent University (77)
    Rivier College (48)
    Rochester Institute of Technology (53)
    Salem State College (30)
    Southern Illinois University at Carbondale (17)
    Southwest Missouri State University (42)
    Spalding University (26)
    St. John's University (54)
    State University of New York at Oswego (55)
    Teachers College of Columbia University (56)
    University of Akron (69)
    University of Dayton (70)
    University of Delaware (10)
    University of Houston (74)
    University of Illinois at Chicago (18)
    University of Illinois at Urbana-Champaign (19)
    University of Iowa (23)
    University of Massachusetts - Boston (31)
    University of Michigan (34)
    University of Missouri - St. Louis (43)
    University of North Carolina - Charlotte (60)
    University of Northern Colorado (8)
    University of Northern Iowa (24)
    University of Texas at Austin (75)
    University of Washington (78)
    University of Wisconsin - Madison (79)
    University of Wisconsin - Stout (80)
    Utah State University (76)
    Washburn University of Topeka (25)
    Wayne State University (35)
    Westfield State College (32)
    Worcester State College (33)

Attitude

    Campbell University (58)

Behavior Assessment

Azusa Pacific University (1)
Baylor University (72)
Bridgewater State College (28)
Buros Institute of Mental Measurements (45)
California Polytechnic State University - San Luis Obispo (2)
California School of Professional Psychology - Fresno (3)
California School of Professional Psychology, Los Angeles Campus (4)
California State University - Chico (5)
California State University - Long Beach (7)
Campbell University (58)
Chicago School of Professional Psychology (13)
Concordia University (Illinois) (15)
Educational Testing Service (49)
Georgia School of Professional Psychology (12)
Harris-Stowe State College (40)
Harvard Graduate School of Education (29)
Kent State University (62)
Minnesota School of Professional Psychology (37)
Mount Saint Mary College (51)
Ohio State University (66)
Plymouth State College (47)
Rivier College (48)
Rochester Institute of Technology (53)
Salem State College (30)
Spalding University (26)
St. John's University (54)
State University of New York at Oswego (55)
Teachers College of Columbia University (56)
University of Akron (69)
University of Delaware (10)
University of Houston (74)
University of Illinois at Urbana-Champaign (19)
University of Nebraska - Kearney (46)
University of North Carolina - Charlotte (60)
University of Northern Colorado (8)
University of Northern Iowa (24)
University of Southern Mississippi (39)
University of Texas at Austin (75)
University of Washington (78)
University of Wisconsin - Stout (80)
Utah State University (76)
Washburn University of Topeka (25)

Behavior Assessment (cont.)
    Westfield State College (32)
    Worcester State College (33)

Bilingual education/second language acquisition
    University of Massachusetts - Boston (31)

Career
    North Carolina State University (59)

Developmental
    Azusa Pacific University (1)
    Baylor University (72)
    Boston College (27)
    Bridgewater State College (28)
    Buros Institute of Mental Measurements (45)
    California School of Professional Psychology - Fresno (3)
    California School of Professional Psychology, Los Angeles Campus (4)
    California State University - Chico (5)
    Campbell University (58)
    Chicago School of Professional Psychology (13)
    Concordia University (Illinois) (15)
    Concordia University (Minnesota) (36)
    Educational Testing Service (49)
    Harris-Stowe State College (40)
    Harvard Graduate School of Education (29)
    Illinois State University (16)
    Kent State University (62)
    Minnesota State University - Mankato (38)
    Mount Saint Mary College (51)
    Ohio State University (66)
    Plymouth State College (47)
    Rivier College (48)
    Salem State College (30)
    Southwest Missouri State University (42)
    Teachers College of Columbia University (56)
    University of Akron (69)
    University of Dayton (70)
    University of Delaware (10)
    University of Houston (74)
    University of Illinois at Chicago (18)
    University of Massachusetts - Boston (31)
    University of Michigan (34)

Developmental (cont.)
    University of Missouri - St. Louis (43)
    University of North Carolina - Charlotte (60)
    University of Northern Colorado (8)
    University of Northern Iowa (24)
    University of Southern Mississippi (39)
    University of Texas at Austin (75)
    University of Wisconsin - Madison (79)
    University of Wisconsin - Stout (80)
    Washburn University of Topeka (25)
    Westfield State College (32)
    Worcester State College (33)

Education
    American College Testing (22)
    Azusa Pacific University (1)
    Baylor University (72)
    Boston College (27)
    Bridgewater State College (28)
    Buros Institute of Mental Measurements (45)
    California Polytechnic State University - San Luis Obispo (2)
    California State University - Chico (5)
    California State University - Long Beach (7)
    Campbell University (58)
    Concordia University (Minnesota) (36)
    Educational Testing Service (49)
    Florida International University (11)
    Harris-Stowe State College (40)
    Harvard Graduate School of Education (29)
    Illinois State University (16)
    Kent State University (62)
    Miami University (64)
    Minnesota State University - Mankato (38)
    Montclair St. University (50)
    Mount Saint Mary College (51)
    Ohio State University (66)
    Plymouth State College (47)
    Regent University (77)
    Rivier College (48)
    Rochester Institute of Technology (53)
    St. John's University (54)
    Teachers College of Columbia University (56)
    Salem State College (30)

Education (cont.)
Southern Illinois University at Carbondale (17)
Southwest Missouri State University (42)
Texas Tech University (73)
University of Akron (69)
University of Dayton (70)
University of Delaware (10)
University of Houston (74)
University of Illinois at Urbana-Champaign (19)
University of Iowa (23)
University of Massachusetts - Boston (31)
University of Michigan (34)
University of Missouri - St. Louis (43)
University of Nebraska - Kearney (46)
University of North Carolina - Charlotte (60)
University of Northern Colorado (8)
University of Northern Iowa (24)
University of Washington (78)
University of Wisconsin - Madison (79)
University of Wisconsin - Stout (80)
Washburn University of Topeka (25)
Western Oregon University (71)
Westfield State College (32)
Worcester State College (33)

English
American College Testing (22)
Buros Institute of Mental Measurements (45)
California State University - Chico (5)
California State University - Long Beach (7)
Campbell University (58)
Educational Testing Service (49)
Florida International University (11)
Harris-Stowe State College (40)
Harvard Graduate School of Education (29)
Montclair St. University (50)
Notre Dame College (Ohio) (65)
Ohio State University (66)
Plymouth State College (47)
Rivier College (48)
Teachers College of Columbia University (56)
University of Dayton (70)
University of Illinois at Chicago (18)

English (cont.)
>University of Illinois at Urbana-Champaign (19)
>University of Massachusetts - Boston (31)
>University of North Carolina - Charlotte (60)
>University of Northern Iowa (24)
>University of Wisconsin - Stout (80)
>Wayne State University (35)
>Worcester State College (33)

English as a Second Language (ESL)
>University of North Carolina - Charlotte (60)

Fine Arts
>Buros Institute of Mental Measurements (45)
>California State University - Chico (5)
>Campbell University (58)
>Educational Testing Service (49)
>Ohio State University (66)
>Plymouth State College (47)
>Teachers College of Columbia University (56)
>University of Northern Iowa (24)
>Worcester State College (33)

Foreign Languages
>Buros Institute of Mental Measurements (45)
>California State University - Chico (5)
>Educational Testing Service (49)
>Montclair St. University (50)
>Plymouth State College (47)
>Teachers College of Columbia University (56)
>University of Illinois at Urbana-Champaign (19)
>University of Massachusetts - Boston (31)

Health
>University of Northern Iowa (24)

Intelligence and Scholastic Aptitude
>American College Testing (22)
>Azusa Pacific University (1)
>Baylor University (72)
>Boston College (27)
>Bridgewater State College (28)
>Buros Institute of Mental Measurements (45)

Intelligence and Scholastic Aptitude (cont.)
    California Polytechnic State University - San Luis Obispo (2)
    California State University - Chico (5)
    Campbell University (58)
    Chicago School of Professional Psychology (13)
    Educational Testing Service (49)
    Harris-Stowe State College (40)
    Harvard Graduate School of Education (29)
    Kent State University (62)
    Minnesota State University - Mankato (38)
    Mount Saint Mary College (51)
    North Carolina State University (59)
    Notre Dame College (Ohio) (65)
    Ohio State University (66)
    Plymouth State College (47)
    Southern Illinois University at Carbondale (17)
    Teachers College of Columbia University (56)
    University of Delaware (10)
    University of Illinois at Urbana-Champaign (19)
    University of Massachusetts - Boston (31)
    University of Michigan (34)
    University of Missouri - St. Louis (43)
    University of North Carolina - Charlotte (60)
    University of Northern Iowa (24)
    University of Wisconsin - Madison (79)
    Wayne State University (35)

Interest Inventories
    Campbell University (58)

Learning Disabilities
    Campbell University (58)

Learning Styles
    University of Dayton (70)

Marital/Family Assessment
    Campbell University (58)

Mathematics
    American College Testing (22)
    Boston College (27)
    Buros Institute of Mental Measurements (45)

Mathematics (cont.)

California State University - Chico (5)
California State University - Long Beach (7)
Educational Testing Service (49)
Florida International University (11)
Harvard Graduate School of Education (29)
Kent State University (62)
Mount Saint Mary College (51)
Notre Dame College (Ohio) (65)
Ohio State University (66)
Plymouth State College (47)
Rivier College (48)
Rochester Institute of Technology (53)
State University of New York at Oswego (55)
Teachers College of Columbia University (56)
University of Dayton (70)
University of Illinois at Chicago (18)
University of Illinois at Urbana-Champaign (19)
University of Massachusetts - Boston (31)
University of Missouri - St. Louis (43)
University of North Carolina - Charlotte (60)
University of Northern Iowa (24)
University of Wisconsin - Stout (80)
Wayne State University (35)
Westfield State College (32)
Worcester State College (33)

Miscellaneous

Baylor University (72)
Buros Institute of Mental Measurements (45)
California State University - Chico (5)
California State University - Long Beach (7)
Campbell University (58)
Concordia University (Illinois) (15)
Educational Testing Service (49)
Illinois State University (16)
Kent State University (62)
Mount Saint Mary College (51)
Ohio State University (66)
Teachers College of Columbia University (56)
University of Illinois at Chicago (18)
University of Illinois at Urbana-Champaign (19)
University of Wisconsin - Stout (80)

Multi-Aptitude Batteries

American College Testing (22)
Azusa Pacific University (1)
Baylor University (72)
Buros Institute of Mental Measurements (45)
California Polytechnic State University - San Luis Obispo (2)
California State University - Chico (5)
Concordia University (Illinois) (15)
Educational Testing Service (49)
Florida International University (11)
Georgia School of Professional Psychology (12)
Harvard Graduate School of Education (29)
Kent State University (62)
Minnesota State University - Mankato (38)
Mount Saint Mary College (51)
Ohio State University (66)
Plymouth State College (47)
Regent University (77)
Rivier College (48)
Rochester Institute of Technology (53)
Salem State College (30)
Spalding University (26)
St. John's University (54)
State University of New York at Oswego (55)
Teachers College of Columbia University (56)
University of Akron (69)
University of Illinois at Urbana-Champaign (19)
University of Iowa (23)
University of Missouri - St. Louis (43)
University of Northern Colorado (8)
University of Northern Iowa (24)
University of Washington (78)
University of Wisconsin - Madison (79)
University of Wisconsin - Stout (80)
Washburn University of Topeka (25)
Westfield State College (32)
Worcester State College (33)

NC Competency Tests

Western Carolina University (61)

Neuropsychological

Boston College (27)
Buros Institute of Mental Measurements (45)
California Polytechnic State University - San Luis Obispo (2)
California School of Professional Psychology - Fresno (3)
California School of Professional Psychology, Los Angeles Campus (4)
California State University - Chico (5)
Campbell University (58)
Chicago School of Professional Psychology (13)
Educational Testing Service (49)
Georgia School of Professional Psychology (12)
Harvard Graduate School of Education (29)
Illinois State University (16)
Minnesota School of Professional Psychology (37)
Montclair St. University (50)
Ohio State University (66)
Regent University (77)
Spalding University (26)
Teachers College of Columbia University (56)
University of Akron (69)
University of Iowa (23)
University of Northern Colorado (8)
University of Wisconsin - Stout (80)
Utah State University (76)
Worcester State College (33)

Personality

Azusa Pacific University (1)
Baylor University (72)
Buros Institute of Mental Measurements (45)
California Polytechnic State University - San Luis Obispo (2)
California School of Professional Psychology - Fresno (3)
California School of Professional Psychology, Los Angeles Campus (4)
California State University - Chico (5)
California State University - Long Beach (7)
Campbell University (58)
Chicago School of Professional Psychology (13)
Concordia University (Illinois) (15)
Educational Testing Service (49)
Florida International University (11)
Georgia School of Professional Psychology (12)
Harvard Graduate School of Education (29)
Illinois State University (16)

Personality (cont.)

    Kent State University (62)
    Minnesota School of Professional Psychology (37)
    Minnesota State University - Mankato (38)
    North Carolina State University (59)
    Ohio State University (66)
    Plymouth State College (47)
    Regent University (77)
    Rivier College (48)
    Rochester Institute of Technology (53)
    Salem State College (30)
    Southern Illinois University at Carbondale (17)
    Spalding University (26)
    St. John's University (54)
    State University of New York at Oswego (55)
    Teachers College of Columbia University (56)
    University of Akron (69)
    University of Dayton (70)
    University of Delaware (10)
    University of Houston (74)
    University of Illinois at Chicago (18)
    University of Illinois at Urbana-Champaign (19)
    University of Iowa (23)
    University of Massachusetts - Boston (31)
    University of Missouri - St. Louis (43)
    University of Nebraska - Kearney (46)
    University of Northern Colorado (8)
    University of Northern Iowa (24)
    University of Texas at Austin (75)
    University of Washington (78)
    University of Wisconsin - Stout (80)
    Utah State University (76)
    Wayne State University (35)
    Western Oregon University (71)
    Worcester State College (33)

Physical Education

    University of Northern Iowa (24)

Reading

    Azusa Pacific University (1)
    Baylor University (72)
    Bridgewater State College (28)

Reading (cont.)

Buros Institute of Mental Measurements (45)
California Polytechnic State University - San Luis Obispo (2)
California State University - Chico (5)
California State University - Long Beach (7)
Campbell University (58)
Chicago State University (14)
Concordia University (Minnesota) (36)
Educational Testing Service (49)
Florida International University (11)
Harris-Stowe State College (40)
Harvard Graduate School of Education (29)
Kent State University (62)
Lake Erie College (63)
Miami University (64)
Montclair St. University (50)
Mount Saint Mary College (51)
Notre Dame College (Ohio) (65)
Ohio State University (66)
Plymouth State College (47)
Regent University (77)
Rivier College (48)
Rochester Institute of Technology (53)
Salem State College (30)
Southwest Missouri State University (42)
Spalding University (26)
St. John's University (54)
State University of New York at Oswego (55)
Teachers College of Columbia University (56)
University of Akron (69)
University of Dayton (70)
University of Illinois at Chicago (18)
University of Illinois at Urbana-Champaign (19)
University of Massachusetts - Boston (31)
University of Michigan (34)
University of Missouri - St. Louis (43)
University of Nebraska - Kearney (46)
University of North Carolina - Charlotte (60)
University of Northern Colorado (8)
University of Northern Iowa (24)
University of Texas at Austin (75)
University of Wisconsin - Madison (79)
University of Wisconsin - Stout (80)

Reading (cont.)

Washburn University of Topeka (25)
Wayne State University (35)
Western Oregon University (71)
Westfield State College (32)
Worcester State College (33)

Science

University of Illinois at Urbana-Champaign (19)
University of Northern Iowa (24)

Sensory Motor

Boston College (27)
Buros Institute of Mental Measurements (45)
California School of Professional Psychology, Los Angeles Campus (4)
California State University - Chico (5)
Campbell University (58)
Chicago School of Professional Psychology (13)
Educational Testing Service (49)
Florida International University (11)
Georgia School of Professional Psychology (12)
Harvard Graduate School of Education (29)
Kent State University (62)
Minnesota State University - Mankato (38)
Mount Saint Mary College (51)
Ohio State University (66)
Plymouth State College (47)
Rivier College (48)
Salem State College (30)
Spalding University (26)
Teachers College of Columbia University (56)
University of Akron (69)
University of Dayton (70)
University of Massachusetts - Boston (31)
University of Michigan (34)
University of Northern Iowa (24)
University of Southern Mississippi (39)
University of Texas at Austin (75)
University of Wisconsin - Stout (80)
Washburn University of Topeka (25)
Worcester State College (33)

Social Studies
Buros Institute of Mental Measurements (45)
California State University - Chico (5)
Educational Testing Service (49)
Florida International University (11)
Harvard Graduate School of Education (29)
Notre Dame College (Ohio) (65)
Ohio State University (66)
Teachers College of Columbia University (56)
University of Illinois at Urbana-Champaign (19)
University of Massachusetts - Boston (31)
University of Northern Iowa (24)
University of Wisconsin - Stout (80)
Worcester State College (33)

Speech and Hearing
Boston College (27)
Bridgewater State College (28)
Buros Institute of Mental Measurements (45)
California Polytechnic State University - San Luis Obispo (2)
California School of Professional Psychology - Fresno (3)
California State University - Chico (5)
Educational Testing Service (49)
Florida International University (11)
Illinois State University (16)
Mount Saint Mary College (51)
Ohio State University (66)
Rivier College (48)
Rochester Institute of Technology (53)
Southwest Missouri State University (42)
Teachers College of Columbia University (56)
University of Massachusetts - Boston (31)
University of Missouri - St. Louis (43)
University of Northern Colorado (8)
University of Northern Iowa (24)
University of Southern Mississippi (39)
University of Texas at Austin (75)
University of Wisconsin - Stout (80)
Worcester State College (33)

Vocations
American College Testing (22)
Azusa Pacific University (1)

Vocations (cont.)
  Baylor University (72)
  Buros Institute of Mental Measurements (45)
  California Polytechnic State University - San Luis Obispo (2)
  California State University - Chico (5)
  Campbell University (58)
  Educational Testing Service (49)
  Harvard Graduate School of Education (29)
  Indiana State University
  Kent State University (62)
  Minnesota State University - Mankato (38)
  North Carolina State University (59)
  Ohio State University (66)
  Plymouth State College (47)
  Rivier College (48)
  St. John's University (54)
  State University of New York at Oswego (55)
  Teachers College of Columbia University (56)
  University of Akron (69)
  University of Illinois at Chicago (18)
  University of Illinois at Urbana-Champaign (19)
  University of Massachusetts - Boston (31)
  University of Missouri - St. Louis (43)
  University of North Carolina - Charlotte (60)
  University of Northern Iowa (24)
  Utah State University (76)
  Wayne State University (35)
  Worcester State College (33)

Directory of Curriculum Materials Centers
Edited by Fred Olive
Compiled by The Curriculum Materials Centers Directory Revision
Ad Hoc Committee of the Education and Behavioral Sciences Section

Many institutions of higher education in the United States and
Canada support their teacher education programs by developing
curriculum materials centers (CMCs) which feature instructional
materials representative of those found in preschool through high
school (PreK-12) settings. The materials often constitute a
separately maintained and housed collection, and are often
adjoined by a media production facility.

This directory, now in its fifth edition, lists and describes curriculum
materials centers or collections at 203 institutions. It provides
information about location, contact information, budgets,
physical space, collection size, staff size, hours of operation,
and other descriptive information.

This electronic edition is designed to provide easy access and to
assist the user in quickly locating a CMC listing by state, by
institution name, or by any other parameter that is desired.

$35.00; ACRL members $31.50

Available online at http://acrl.telusys.com/cmc/index.html

Association of College
& Research Libraries
A Division of the American Library Association